Creative Sermon Starters

D1712846

Group® LOVELAND, COLORADO

Group's R.E.A.L. Guarantee to you:

Every Group resource incorporates our R.E.A.L. approach to ministry—a unique philosophy that results in long-term retention and life transformation. It's ministry that's:

Relational
Because student-to-student interaction enhances learning and builds Christian friendships.

Experiential
Because what students experience sticks with them up to 9 times longer than what they simply hear or read.

Applicable
Because the aim of Christian education is to be both hearers and doers of the Word.

Learner-based
Because students learn more and retain it longer when the process is designed according to how they learn best.

CREATIVE SERMON STARTERS

Visit our Web site: **www.grouppublishing.com**

Credits
Authors: E. Paul Allen, Jim Kochenburger, Kristi Rector, Lana Jo McLaughlin, Jan Kershner, Paul Woods, Pamela J. Shoup, Lori Haynes Niles, Amy Simpson, Trevor Simpson, Les Shelton
Editor: Michael D. Warden
Creative Development Editor: Jim Kochenburger
Chief Creative Officer: Joani Schultz
Copy Editor: Shirley Michaels
Art Director: Kari K. Monson
Cover Art Director: Jeff A. Storm
Cover Designer: Becky Hawley
Cover Photographer: Tony Stone Images
Computer Graphic Artist: Nighthawk Design
Production Manager: Alex Jorgensen

Library of Congress Cataloging-in-Publication Data
    Creative sermon starters.
        p. cm.
        ISBN 0-7644-2139-5
        1. Preaching--Audio-visual aids. 2. Homiletical illustrations. I. Group publishing.

    DV422 .C74 2000
    251'.08--dc21
                                                            99-043810

10 9 8 7 6 5 4 3 2   09 08 07 06 05 04 03 02 01
Printed in the United States of America.

CONTENTS

INTRODUCTION

Hold on to your chair! The following information may shock you: Listeners retain very little of what they hear!

That's right. According to Communication Briefings, people forget 40 percent of what they hear within twenty minutes, 60 percent within a half day, and 90 percent within a week. Regardless of the speaker's skill, most listeners quickly forget the message—and therefore never apply it.

Sound unbelievable? That's understandable. It can be difficult to accept that the primary teaching tool used in churches today—straight lecture—is often the least effective way to help people learn. No wonder many preachers and teachers often feel frustrated in their efforts to help people grow in Christian faith!

In times past, powerful preaching provided a solid foundation for teaching and exhorting people in the church. But times have changed, or, more specifically, *culture* has changed. With the onset of the technological revolution, people have become trained to process information differently. We no longer grasp concepts and lessons by passively listening to a knowledgeable speaker. We're a multimedia culture now, and our learning has, by necessity, become multimedia-based. We need to be "hands on" in our learning. We need to experience the lesson we're trying to learn.

Does that mean you should stop preaching altogether? Hardly. Teaching in a public forum is still a great way to reach large numbers with your message. But your speaking has to adapt to the times. You have to connect with people where they live—in a multifaceted, multifocused, multimedia world. People want to do more than simply listen to a sermon: They want to actively participate in it.

Because you're reading this, you probably already recognize the importance of incorporating elements of active and interactive learning into your sermons. You know the best way for people to learn anything is through experience, not lecture. And learning through experience is what this book is all about.

Creative Sermon Starters provides the resources you need to incorporate participatory and experiential learning into your sermons. The creative ideas aren't designed to replace your sermons, just to strengthen their impact. As you begin to incorporate some of these ideas into your preaching, you'll immediately notice a change in your congregation. You'll find them talking about the experiences you provide for weeks after the event. And, more importantly, you'll notice that they're *learning* from your teaching in ways you never expected.

The book is divided into three sections: video clips, activities, and stories. Once you try any one of these ideas, you'll discover just how easy they are to use. Each activity, video clip, or story is easy to use and usually requires minimal preparation. For maximum effectiveness, you'll want to have your congregations discuss the questions provided in pairs, trios, or foursomes. In this way, each person will be an active participant and will build relationships during the worship time. A great way to wrap up the discussion is to invite a few people to share with the entire congregation the insights they discussed in their group.

Movie clips provide a great opportunity for your people to see the connection between faith and culture. The clips have been carefully selected for all ages, and most of them come from movies that are rated G or PG. Some of the movies chosen might have scenes that would not be appropriate for viewing in church. You might choose to preface the showing of a clip from a movie that is rated PG-13 or R with a warning to parents that you are not recommending the whole movie for family viewing.

Fair use copyright law permits the use of small segments of material for educational purposes. If your church is interested in receiving copyright permission for the use of movie clips, you can contact the Motion Picture Licensing Corporation at (800) 462-8855 and receive an annual license for a very modest fee.

Times have changed. Learning has changed. So let your teaching change, too. It's as easy as picking an activity, video clip, or story, and giving it a try. You'll be surprised how well it works. And, even better, your congregation will never be the same.

Section 1:
CREATIVE MOVIE CLIPS

TITLE: *Angels in the Endzone* (Walt Disney Television)

THEME: Friends

SCRIPTURE: Proverbs 15:33

Related Passages: Proverbs 12:26; Galatians 6:7; Ephesians 4:17-19; and 1 Thessalonians 5:4-6

Overview: Jesse realizes that his friends aren't who he thought they were. He demonstrates his own character by choosing to walk away rather than to engage in a sinful act.

Start Time: about 1 hour, 6 minutes into the movie

Start Cue: A car pulls into a gas station.

End Time: about 1 hour, 9 minutes into the movie

End Cue: Bodean gets back into the car after being confronted by Jesse.

Comments: Other parts of this movie contain material that may not be appropriate for family viewing.

Application: Before watching the video, read Proverbs 15:33. After the clip, discuss how and why bad company corrupts good character. In your discussion, encourage your listeners to consider these questions:

- **In what ways do adults face peer pressure?**
- **When have you stood up to negative peer pressure and done the right thing? What was the result?**
- **What are some attributes of a friend with good character?**
- **What should you do about unavoidable "bad company," such as negative work or family situations?**

TITLE: *Anne of Green Gables* (Walt Disney Home Video)

THEME: Appearance

SCRIPTURE: Matthew 6:28-30

Related Passages: 1 Samuel 16:7; Matthew 23:27-28; and James 2:1-12

Overview: Anne laments over the fact that she can't be perfectly happy because her hair is red. She wonders if it's best to be beautiful, good, or smart.

Start Time: about 18 minutes into the movie

Start Cue: Anne says, "Dreams don't often come true, do they, Mr. Cuthbert?"

End Time: about 19 minutes into the movie

End Cue: Matthew Cuthbert says, "I don't know."

Comments: A movie classic.

Application: Ask the congregation, **"If there was one thing you could change about your appearance, what would it be?"** Then briefly talk through an example of a typical day, explaining how much time a person might take to work on appearance. For example, you might spend thirty minutes doing your hair, putting on makeup, or shaving; ten minutes picking out clothes and getting dressed; and so on. Ask the people to roughly estimate the total time each day they work on their appearance.

Then read John 7:24, and discuss the importance of spending time working on the "appearance" of their hearts (through Bible study, prayer, and service) and not just the appearance of their bodies.

TITLE: *Antz* (Dream Works SKG)

THEME: Sharing faith

SCRIPTURE: 1 Peter 3:15

Overview: The main character of the story, a young ant, is struggling with finding a better way of life. An old grandfather-type ant tries to tell him about a special place he's seen, but everyone makes fun of the old ant.

Start Time: about 11 minutes into the movie

Start Cue: The main character ant, Z-4195, says, "There's just got to be a better place."

End Time: a little over 12 minutes into the movie

End Cue: Friend ant laughs loudly and says, "Dream on, Z."

Comments: Though this video is animated, it addresses several adult issues.

Application: Use this clip to lead into a message on how difficult it can sometimes be to share our faith. In your discussion, read 1 Peter 3:15, and encourage listeners to consider these questions:

- **How was the behavior of the ants similar to the way people act when you try to share your faith?**
- **How were Z's comments similar to those of troubled people you know?**
- **How might 1 Peter 3:15 help you learn how to respond when people ridicule your faith?**

....

TITLE: *At First Sight* (MGM)
THEME: Disappointments
SCRIPTURE: Hebrews 11:1
Related Passages: Matthew 9:29; Romans 1:12; and 2 Corinthians 5:7
Overview: Architect Amy Benic has decided to take a break from her busy schedule in New York. She goes to a lodge and meets a blind man named Virgil Adamson. She's attracted to Virgil and finds out about a procedure that would allow him to see again. She speaks with Virgil's sister, Jenny, regarding the surgery.

Start Time: about 40 minutes into the movie
Start Cue: Amy says, "Could I speak to you for a minute?"
End Time: a little over 41 minutes into the movie
End Cue: Jenny, says, "I learned a long time ago to stop believing in miracles."

Application: Begin with the video clip, then read Hebrews 11:1. Immediately after Jenny's statement in the clip, she says that her father had brought in all kinds of people to try to heal her brother's eyesight. She said it almost destroyed her family and almost killed her brother. Point out that we often feel disappointed and lose faith in God when we have tried to do everything we know of to correct a situation, and nothing works. Discuss how to hold onto faith in the midst of disappointment. In your discussion, encourage listeners to consider these questions:
- **When have you lost faith in God?**
- **How did you overcome your disappointment (if you did)?**
- **How can faith stay strong even when disappointments come?**

TITLE: *Beauty and the Beast* (Walt Disney Productions)
THEME: Judging others
SCRIPTURE: 1 Samuel 16:7

Related Passages: Proverbs 31:30; Matthew 23:27; 1 Timothy 2:9-10; and
1 Peter 3:3-5

Overview: This is a fairy tale about a prince who was turned into a beast because he was selfish and cruel and a girl who was able to see past his
appearance to the good that was inside him.

Start Time: about 30 seconds into the movie
Start Cue: The narrator says, "Once upon a time…"
End Time: about 1.5 minutes into the movie
End Cue: The narrator says, "…and all who lived there."
Comments: Although this video is animated, it addresses several adult themes.

Application: Show the video clip, then use the following questions to
prompt listeners to think about appearances:
- **Why is it so hard to see past a person's outer appearance to the good
qualities about his or her character?**
- **What would it be like if we saw each other as God sees us?**

Briefly describe the story of David's call to become king, and read 1 Samuel
16:7. Lead into your sermon by discussing how God ignores the outward appearance and looks at the heart.

TITLE: *Beauty and the Beast* (Walt Disney Productions)
THEME: Pride
SCRIPTURE: Luke 18:9-14

Related Passages: Romans 15:17; Proverbs 11:2; and Proverbs 18:12
Overview: Gaston sings about how wonderful he thinks he is and how Belle
would be a lucky girl to marry someone as handsome as he.

Start Time: about 6 minutes into the movie
Start Cue: Belle crosses the courtyard, and a flock of geese fly across the sky.

End Time: about 9 minutes into the movie

End Cue: Belle takes her book from Gaston, saying, "I have to get home to help my father."

Comments: Although this video is animated, it addresses several adult themes.

Application: Use Luke 18:9-14 as a contrast between pride and humility. Then show the video clip, and encourage listeners to consider the following questions:

- **How much of Gaston do you see in yourself?**
- **After reading Luke 18:9-14, what do Gaston and the Pharisee have in common?**
- **When have you been like the Pharisee?**
- **When have you been like the tax collector?**
- **Which one would you feel most comfortable being around? Why?**

TITLE: *Charlotte's Web* (Paramount Pictures)

THEME: Our value to God

SCRIPTURE: Psalm 139:13-16

Related Passages: 1 Corinthians 12:18-22 and Galatians 3:26-28

Overview: Fern and her father discuss whether or not to kill a pig because it is a runt and has no value.

Start Time: about 4 minutes into the movie

Start Cue: Fern walks past her father and says, "Good morning, papa."

End Time: about 6 minutes into the movie

End Cue: Papa hands Fern a baby pig, and she says, "Look at him, he's absolutely perfect."

Comments: Although this video is animated, it addresses several adult themes.

Application: After showing the video clip, encourage listeners to consider the following questions about our value as people:

- **What did Fern value in the runt that her father didn't?**
- **In our culture, whom do we consider the runts of our society?**
- **In what ways are they considered of less value?**

Continue your sermon by reading Psalm 139:13-16 and stressing the value of those people that society considers to be less valuable.

TITLE: *Contact* (Warner Bros.)

THEME: Nature of faith

SCRIPTURE: Hebrews 11:1-3

Related Passages: 2 Corinthians 5:7; Hebrews 11:6; and 1 Peter 1:8-9

Overview: Jodie Foster plays a scientist whose father died when she was young. She trusts only facts and things that she can see. Matthew McConaughey plays a religious man who believes in faith. He uses her love for her father to explain why it's possible to believe in something that can't be proven.

Start Time: about 1 hour, 12 minutes into the movie

Start Cue: Matthew McConaughey walks up to Jodie Foster at a party and says, "Wow, you look beautiful."

End Time: about 1 hour, 15 minutes into the movie

End Cue: McConaughey says, "Prove it," and Foster's pager rings.

Comments: The two characters are drinking glasses of champagne as the scene is carried out.

Application: After showing the video clip, discuss whether it's possible to prove that God exists. Read Hebrews 11:1-3, and encourage listeners to consider how developing a personal relationship with God is a type of "proof" for his existence, since it is a form of "evidence" of something we can't see. You might also encourage listeners to consider these questions:

- **How would you prove that your father or mother existed to someone who had never seen him or her?**
- **How is that similar to how we should respond to people who challenge us to prove God exists?**
- **What does it mean to demonstrate faith in God, since we can't see him?**

TITLE: *Dead Poets Society* (Touchstone Pictures)

THEME: Making life count

SCRIPTURE: Psalm 39:4-7

Related Passages: Psalm 49:10-15; Jeremiah 10:23; Matthew 16:25; Romans 6:13; and 1 John 3:14

Overview: An unorthodox teacher (Robin Williams) leaves his students with an unforgettable impression when he challenges them to seize the day and make their lives extraordinary.

Start Time: about 14 minutes into the movie

Start Cue: Students enter the classroom of their new teacher, John Keating.

End Time: about 17 minutes into the movie

End Cue: The teacher whispers to the boys, "Carpe deum...seize the day, boys...make your lives extraordinary."

Comments: Other parts of this movie contain material that may not be appropriate for family viewing.

Application: Show the video clip. Point out how this teacher placed the mortality of these young men before them to get them to take a look at what their lives were all about. Read Psalm 39:4-7. Then lead a short discussion by asking these questions:

- **How does looking at our own mortality help us to put our priorities in perspective?**
- **Why is it important to occasionally look at our lives like this?**
- **What does "seize the day" mean for Christians?**
- **What do you believe to be an extraordinary Christian life?**
- **If, at your funeral, someone were to sum up your life in a single sentence, what would you most want him or her to say? Why?**

TITLE: *Ever After* (20th Century Fox)

THEME: Servanthood

SCRIPTURE: Matthew 25:34-40

Related Passages: Matthew 20:26-28 and Luke 14:7-11; 22:24-27

Overview: Based on the fairy tale *Cinderella*, this scene shows Danielle serving her stepmother and stepsisters graciously, despite the fact that they put her down and treat her with disdain.

Start Time: about 17 minutes into the movie

Start Cue: Danielle says, "Good morning, madam."

End Time: about 18 minutes into the movie

End Cue: The stepmother says, "Calm down, child. Relax."

Comments: Other parts of this movie contain material that may not be appropriate for family viewing.

Application: After showing the video clip, encourage listeners to consider these questions:

- **What's your typical reaction when you're put in a position to serve others?**
- **How does the way a person treats you affect your attitude toward serving him or her?**

Read Matthew 25:34-40. Explain that God calls us to be humble, serving each other with love—even when others don't treat us well. As we serve others, we serve God also.

TITLE: *Fiddler on the Roof* (United Artists)

THEME: Persecution for faith

SCRIPTURE: 1 Peter 4:16

Related Passages: Matthew 5:44 and Luke 21:12-19

Overview: The Russian Jews of Anatevka are being forced to leave their homes with three days' notice as the Russians try to clear the district of all Jewish people.

Start Time: about 2 hours, 54 minutes into the movie

Start Cue: The constable rides up to where the Jewish men are gathered in the village.

End Time: about 2 hours, 57 minutes into the movie

End Cue: One man comments that this wouldn't be a good time for the Messiah to come, and the rabbi replies, "We'll have to wait for him somewhere else."

Comments: Although this movie deals with the Jewish faith, it's a wonderful story about one man's personal relationship with God, his joy in his faith, and the suffering he endures for it.

Application: Use this clip to talk about Christians suffering ridicule from other people, the media, or society in general, while continuing to witness boldly. In this discussion, highlight Christians who are physically, mentally, and socially persecuted and even die for their faith in non-Christian countries around the world, such as China, India, and the Middle East. You could even share stories from missionaries in your church or in your denomination. During your discussion, encourage listeners to consider these questions:

- **How does persecution in this country compare with persecution in other countries?**
- **Is persecution good for Christianity? Why or why not?**
- **What degree of persecution would you be willing to endure for your faith? Why?**

TITLE: *The Flintstones* (Universal Pictures)

THEME: Marriage relationship

SCRIPTURE: Ephesians 5:22-28

Related Passages: Colossians 3:15-19 and 1 Peter 3:5-7

Overview: Fred has just come home from work and Wilma welcomes him. Then they get into an argument about money, and Fred announces that he is the "king of this cave."

Start Time: about 7 minutes, 18 seconds into the movie

Start Cue: Fred is sitting in his chair. Wilma says," It does my heart good to see you relaxing after a hard day at the quarry."

End Time: about 8 minutes, 40 seconds into the movie

End Cue: Fred says, "And you have every right to know, my queen."

Comments: Just prior to this scene, Fred makes a couple of crude remarks and then asks for a "brew." These may be offensive to some people, so be careful not to start the clip too early. Also, at the end of the clip, the story goes a different direction than expected and would take away from the impact of the clip if allowed to run past the indicated end cue.

Application: This clip would be great to introduce a sermon on healthy marriage relationships. After showing the clip, encourage listeners to consider these questions:

- **How much have things changed since these mythical "cave man" days?**
- **What about this exchange is similar to what has taken place in your home lately?**
- **How are the attitudes demonstrated here detrimental to a good husband-wife relationship?**

Read Ephesians 5:22-28 as you lead into the sermon.

··

TITLE: *For Richer or Poorer* (Universal Pictures)

THEME: Integrity

SCRIPTURE: 1 John 1:5-10

Related Passages: John 3:19-21; 1 Corinthians 3:18-19; and James 1:22-25

Overview: Brad, who has been pretending to be Amish to hide from the law, is with Samuel, a devout Amish, in a cornfield they planted. They discuss what is real and talk about who are the ones who are really hiding.

Start Time: about 1 hour, 23 minutes into the movie

Start Cue: A cornfield comes on the screen, then Brad says, "This is unbelievable."

End Time: just over 1 hour, 24 minutes into the movie

End Cue: Brad says, "It's those English...always hiding."

Application: Set up this clip by telling a bit of the preceding story: Brad, played by Tim Allen, is a high-powered executive who has been hiding out in an Amish colony for several weeks to escape legal problems. But the simple, devout lifestyle of the Amish has begun to have an effect on him.

After the clip, encourage listeners to consider these questions:

- **How do we know what is real?**
- **What kinds of things are we hiding in our lives?**
- **What does it mean to have integrity about who you are?**

....

TITLE: *Forrest Gump* (Paramount Pictures)

THEME: Miracles

SCRIPTURE: Psalm 77:14

Related Passages: Acts 19:11; John 2:1-11; and John 11:38-44

Overview: The young Forrest Gump is mentally slow, wears leg braces for a crooked back, and is ridiculed by his peers—except for Jenny, his best friend. Sitting at a bus stop as an adult, Forrest reminisces about a miracle in his life.

Start Time: just over 15 minutes into the movie

Start Cue: Forrest tells the woman on the park bench, "My momma always told me that miracles happen every day."

End Time: just over 17 minutes into the movie

End Cue: Forrest runs off through the field.

Comments: This clip actually addresses a variety of other themes as well, including encouragement from a friend, bullies, and belief in oneself.

Application: Forrest saw a miracle as God helped him throw off his braces and gave him the courage and ability to run like the wind. Ask church members about miracles that they have seen in their own lives and how those miracles testify to God's great power and love for us. Close out the sharing time by reading Psalm 77:14.

TITLE: *Hope Floats* (20th Century Fox)

THEME: Joy in time of sorrow

SCRIPTURE: James 1:2-4

Related Passages: Matthew 5:1-12 and John 16:20-24

Overview: A series of scenes accompany the song "Smile."

Start Time: about 35 minutes into the movie

Start Cue: A waitress brings food to Birdee in restaurant.

End Time: about 38 minutes into the movie

End Cue: Birdee develops pictures in the darkroom.

Comments: Other parts of this movie contain material that may not be appropriate for family viewing.

Application: Read James 1:2-4, then lead into a discussion of how we can experience joy in the midst of trials or sorrow. Show the video clip, and encourage listeners to consider these questions:

- **At what times in your life have you found it difficult to find any joy in life?**
- **What are some practical ways to go about experiencing joy in times of sorrow?**
- **In James 1:2-4, James doesn't say to be joyful *if* you experience troubles but *when* you face them. What point is he trying to make in this passage?**
- **Why is it important to have joy even in times of sorrow?**

Continue your sermon, discussing how our trials and times of sorrow can teach perseverance and deepen our faith.

TITLE: *Indiana Jones and the Last Crusade* (Paramount Pictures)

THEME: Faith

SCRIPTURE: Matthew 17:20

Related Passage: Hebrews 11:1-40

Overview: Indiana Jones follows the Nazis to the location of the Holy Grail, the cup of Jesus Christ. Indiana's father has been wounded, forcing Indiana to brave the traps that have kept the grail secret, since only the healing power of the grail can save his father.

Start Time: about 1 hour, 44 minutes into the movie

Start Cue: Indiana is climbing the steps, reading the first clue: "The penitent man will pass."

End Time: about 1 hour, 48 minutes into the movie

End Cue: Indiana throws dirt over the stone bridge to make it visible.

Comments: The opening scene shows a trap of swords and blades. If you feel this is too scary for young children, start the tape a little later, as Indiana reads about the "leap from the lion's head."

You could also use this clip to talk about Abraham, Moses, David, and other faith heroes of the Bible in Hebrews 11 and relate those to modern-day heroes of the faith.

Application: The final scene is a powerful visual about relying on faith to do what seems impossible. Share times in your life when you have had to rely only on your faith in God to accomplish a difficult task or face a seemingly hopeless situation. Ask church members about a time when they had to rely on their faith in God. Encourage them to consider these questions:

• **Why does God demand faith from his people?**

• **What are common ways God tests our faith?**

• **How should we respond to faith tests?**

....

TITLE: *It's a Wonderful Life* (Republic Pictures, Liberty Films)

THEME: Spiritual gifts

SCRIPTURE: 1 Corinthians 12:1-11

Related Passages: Romans 12:3-8 and 1 Peter 4:10-11

Overview: George Bailey contemplates suicide after Uncle Billy has misplaced $8,000 from the family's savings and loan business. George knows he'll be out of business if he doesn't find the money. Desperate, he prepares to jump off a bridge, but his guardian angel, Clarence, jumps first, forcing

George to save him instead. George wishes he had never been born, and Clarence gives him the opportunity to see what a difference he has made in the lives of many people.

Start Time: about 1 hour, 40 minutes into the movie

Start Cue: Clarence is asked where he comes from and replies, "Heaven."

End Time: about 1 hour, 44 minutes into the movie

End Cue: Clarence closes the door, which has blown up, and speaks to heaven: "You don't have to make all that fuss about it."

Comments: This clip could also be used to illustrate "answers to prayer," since George comments that all he got for his prayer was a busted lip. But the angel says, "I'm the answer to your prayer."

Application: This movie illustrates the good that one person can do with the gifts God has given him or her. It's an excellent theme to lead into a sermon on spiritual gifts, discussing how we all have very different gifts from the Holy Spirit and make different contributions in our lives—some that we're not even aware of. As you lead the discussion, encourage listeners to consider these questions:

- **Why do people sometimes feel as though their lives don't make a difference in the world?**
- **What should we do when we feel as though our lives don't matter?**
- **Do you know what your spiritual gifts are? Why or why not?**
- **How can you start making a difference in someone's life today?**

TITLE: *Liar Liar* (Universal)

THEME: Honesty

SCRIPTURE: Matthew 12:30

Related Passages: Exodus 20:16; Proverbs 14:25; Proverbs 15:4; and 1 Peter 3:10

Overview: Five-year-old Max makes a birthday wish that his unethical lawyer father won't be able to tell a lie for one day. The wish comes true and causes his dad all kinds of problems. The father asks Max to undo the wish.

Start Time: about 38 minutes into the movie

Start Cue: The father (Jim Carrey) asks the kindergarten teacher if he can borrow his son, Max, for a minute.

End Time: just over 40 minutes into the movie

End Cue: A school bell rings and Max's teacher calls him in from recess.

Comments: Other parts of this movie contain material that may not be appropriate for family viewing.

Application: Begin your sermon by talking about the many uses of our tongues—tasting, talking, and guarding us from swallowing things that could choke us. Then talk about how powerful the tongue is—with one small organ we have the power to build someone up with encouraging words or completely destroy a relationship with untrue words. Then show the movie clip and talk about the cost of being honest. Encourage listeners to consider these questions:

- **How can honesty get you into trouble?**
- **Why does God want us to be honest?**
- **Are there times when it's OK to be dishonest? Why or why not?**

TITLE: *The Lion King* (Walt Disney Productions)

THEME: Failure

SCRIPTURE: Colossians 1:13-14

Related Passage: Romans 6:1-3

Overview: Simba (a lion) has a conversation with Rafiki (a baboon) about overcoming failure.

Start Time: about 1 hour, 18 minutes into the movie

Start Cue: Simba sits on the grass and looks at the stars.

End Time: just over 1 hour, 19 minutes into the movie

End Cue: Simba walks off and says, "I'm going back."

Comments: Though this video is animated, it addresses several adult issues.

Application: You can use this clip to introduce a sermon on failure and starting over in Christ. After showing the video clip, encourage listeners to consider these questions about failure:

- **What's one lesson you have learned from a past failure or mistake?**
- **In what ways can the sins or failures of our past become the light of our future?**
- **How can the forgiveness of Christ lead us from failure to freedom?**

Continue your sermon discussing how Christ's forgiveness gives us new opportunities. We no longer are bound to our past sins and failures.

....

TITLE: *The Lion King* (Walt Disney Productions)
THEME: God's forgiveness
SCRIPTURE: 1 John 1:9
Related Passages: Psalm 130:3-4; Micah 7:18-19; and Colossians 3:13
Overview: Simba (a lion) is being punished by his father for going to a place in the pride land where his father had forbidden him to go.

Start Time: about 22 minutes into the movie
Start Cue: Mufasa, the lion king, growls and three hyenas run away.
End Time: just over 24 minutes into the movie
End Cue: Simba says, "We're pals, right?"
Comments: Though this video is animated, it addresses several adult issues.

Application: After showing the video clip, ask listeners to think about a time when someone wronged them. Ask them to consider how easy or difficult it was to forgive that person and whether they thought of ways they'd like to "punish" the offender. Then have them remember a time when they wronged someone else and had to ask for forgiveness. Encourage listeners to consider these questions:

- **How did you feel when that person forgave you?**
- **Why is forgiveness so hard for us to give or receive?**
- **How is the way God forgives different from the way we do?**

Then talk about how God will always forgive us, but unlike humans, he then forgets all of the sins we've committed.

TITLE: *Mother* (Paramount Pictures)

THEME: Marriage

SCRIPTURE: Genesis 2:24

Related Passages: Matthew 19:4-6 and Ephesians 5:22-33

Overview: Jeff's mother has called to tell him that she won't be coming to visit this weekend because her other son, John, is staying with her. Jeff is very upset over the news, and his wife asks him why his world seems to be ending simply because his mother won't be coming.

Start Time: about 1 hour, 10 minutes into the movie

Start Cue: The man says, "I'm not a mama's boy."

End Time: about 1 hour, 11 minutes

End Cue: The wife says, "You just cling more."

Comments: There is some inappropriate language just before this clip, so be sure to cue it up accurately.

Application: You can use this video clip as a lighthearted, humorous approach to the topics of marriage and family relationships. After showing the clip, read Genesis 2:24, and discuss how the man in the video had failed to fully "leave and cleave" in the way the Bible instructs. Encourage listeners to consider these questions:

- **What are some common ways husbands struggle with following God's command to "leave and cleave"?**
- **What are some common ways wives struggle with this issue?**
- **Why is God's command in Genesis 2:24 important?**

TITLE: *Mr. Holland's Opus* (Hollywood Pictures)

THEME: True success

SCRIPTURE: Joshua 1:7-8

Related Passages: 1 Chronicles 22:11-13; 2 Chronicles 26:5; 2 Thessalonians 1:11-12; and 2 Timothy 4:7-8

Overview: Teacher Glenn Holland is being honored for his thirty years of teaching music before the program was cut. Past and present students gather to thank him for impacting their lives.

Start Time: just over 2 hours, 10 minutes into the movie
Start Cue: The female speaker says, "Yes, Principal Wolters, I brought a note from my mother."
End Time: about 2 hours, 12 minutes into the movie
End Cue: The audience applauds.
Comments: Other parts of this movie contain material that may not be appropriate for family viewing.

Application: The week before your sermon, collect objects that might represent the world's view of success. Examples might include a briefcase, a bank statement, jewelry, car keys, a cell phone or beeper, or a small computer pad. Begin your sermon by holding up the objects and describing what kind of person the world calls successful. Then show the movie clip, and read Joshua 1:7-8 to show how success might look from God's point of view.

....

TITLE: *The Parent Trap* (Walt Disney Productions)
THEME: God, our Father
SCRIPTURE: 2 Corinthians 6:18
Related Passages: Matthew 6:9; John 6:46 and 10:30; and Romans 4:11
Overview: Hallie, a California girl, and Annie, a young lady from London, meet accidentally at a summer camp and realize they're identical twins. They decide to switch places so they each can meet the parent they've never known. Not only do they pull it off, they also find a way to reunite their parents.

Start Time: about 48 minutes into the movie
Start Cue: The man says to the girl, "And why do you keep saying 'Dad' at the end of every sentence?"
End Time: about 49 minutes into the movie
End Cue: The two actors look at each other and smile, then the girl looks ahead.
Comments: This particular scene and sermon would fit well with Father's Day.

Whenever you use it, make sure you're sensitive to those in your congregation who don't have fathers.

Application: Before showing the clip, talk about how many people in your church don't have a clear picture of God. They see him either as a removed being in heaven or an uncaring judge. Explain how Scripture can lead you into helping your congregation to understand how God is a loving and concerned Father.

Show the video clip, and read 2 Corinthians 6:18. Just as Annie expresses her reason for calling her father "Dad" and talks about what it would be like to be without a father, you can talk to your congregation about what it's like for those who don't have a relationship with God. Encourage listeners to consider these questions:

- **What would you say to someone who has a negative picture of God as "Father"?**
- **How can you improve your own understanding of God as your Father?**

TITLE: *Pinocchio* (Walt Disney Home Video)
THEME: Truthfulness
SCRIPTURE: Psalm 34:12-13
Related Passages: Proverbs 10:10, 11:3, and 15:1
Overview: Pinocchio's nose grows as he continues to tell a lie.

Start Time: about 48 minutes into the movie
Start Cue: A fairy appears as Pinocchio is looking between his legs.
End Time: just over 49 minutes into the movie
End Cue: Pinocchio says, "I'll never lie again—honest I won't."
Comments: Though this video is animated, it addresses several adult issues.

Application: This video provides a good opportunity to discuss the ethics of lying, such as, "Are there times when telling a lie is acceptable?" As you introduce this topic, encourage listeners to consider these questions:

- **Pinocchio's nose grew longer whenever he lied. While this isn't a typical human characteristic when lying, what are some negative effects humans experience from telling a lie?**

- **Explain what the clip meant by "a lie keeps on growing and growing."**
- **Are there ever times when it's acceptable to tell a lie? Why or why not?**

....

TITLE: *Renaissance Man* (Touchstone Pictures)

THEME: Welcoming visitors

SCRIPTURE: 1 Corinthians 9:19-23

Related Passages: Ephesians 5:15-17 and James 2:1-9

Overview: Danny DeVito is new on the military base and isn't treated kindly. Others speak to him in language that's hard for him to understand.

Start Time: about 18 minutes into the movie

Start Cue: "Welcome to Fort McLane" sign comes into view.

End Time: about 20 minutes into the movie

End Cue: Danny DeVito says, "Can I buy a vowel?"

Comments: Other parts of this movie contain material that may not be appropriate for family viewing.

Application: After showing the video, encourage listeners to consider these questions:

- **When have you been in a new situation or place where you were confused and didn't understand what the people around you were talking about?**
- **In what ways do our own church traditions, language, and behavior make seekers and guests feel uncomfortable?**
- **How can we make our church more seeker-friendly and comfortable for guests?**

Continue your sermon, using 1 Corinthians 9:19-23 as a "launch point" to discuss the importance of reaching out to new people where they are instead of expecting them to immediately feel comfortable in a new situation.

TITLE: *Robin Hood* (Warner Bros.)

THEME: Sin nature

SCRIPTURE: Romans 3:23

Related Passages: Proverbs 20:9; Ecclesiastes 7:20; and 1 John 1:8-10

Overview: Robin Hood is lamenting over the death of his friend and the impending punishment of some of the outlaws he is leading.

Start Time: about 1 hour, 47 minutes into the movie

Start Cue: Two men lay their dead friend on the ground.

End Time: about 1 hour, 48 minutes into the movie

End Cue: Morgan Freeman says, "…only perfect intentions."

Comments: Be aware that just before this scene, the Sheriff of Nottingham is preparing to hang some of Robin Hood's outlaw friends.

Application: Show this clip, then talk about the moral flaws we all struggle to overcome. Read Romans 3:23, and encourage listeners to consider these questions:

- **Do you think we really do always have "perfect intentions"? Why or why not?**
- **Why can't we as humans ever be perfect?**
- **Why can't we save ourselves from sin?**

TITLE: *School Ties* (Paramount Pictures)

THEME: Honoring God

SCRIPTURE: Philippians 1:27

Related Passages: Proverbs 20:11; Romans 12:10; and Ephesians 4:1-3

Overview: A prep school professor is rebuking his class after discovering that one of the students cheated on a test.

Start Time: about 1 hour, 28 minutes into the movie

Start Cue: Students are talking in a classroom before class starts, and the professor walks in.

End Time: about 1 hour, 29 minutes into the movie

End Cue: The professor says, "I leave it in your hands, gentlemen."

Comments: Other parts of this movie contain material that may not be appropriate for family viewing.

Application: Read Philippians 1:27, then ask:

• **What does it mean to live in a manner worthy of the gospel?**

Ask listeners to raise their hands if they have ever murdered someone, mugged a tourist, robbed a bank, or vandalized a neighborhood. Ask whether avoiding these crimes is all there is to living in a manner worthy of the gospel. Then show the clip, and encourage listeners to consider these questions:

• **Cheating isn't as bad as murdering someone, right? So why should we worry about such "small" betrayals of the gospel?**

• **How does every small action we take in life reveal our attitude toward the gospel?**

Point out how we can live in a way that honors God, even through little things, such as taking a test, driving during rush hour, or charging honest prices for our work.

TITLE: *Sister Act* (Touchstone Pictures)

THEME: Prayer

SCRIPTURE: Matthew 6:5-15

Related Passages: Romans 8:26-27; 1 Thessalonians 5:17-18; and James 5:13-16

Overview: After witnessing a crime, the police hide Deloris from gangsters in a convent where she is disguised as Sister Mary Clarence. Deloris, a nightclub singer, is uncomfortable in a nun's habit, but she agrees to a request to pray aloud before a community meal.

Start Time: about 23 minutes into the movie

Start Cue: The nuns gather around the table for lunch, and Mother Superior introduces Sister Mary Clarence.

End Time: just over 24 minutes into the movie

End Cue: Sister Mary Clarence completes her prayer.

Comments: There are many other wonderful scenes in the movie about praising God through music.

Application: After reading the passage, ask listeners to consider the ways they should *not* pray, for example, boasting to God or withholding forgiveness from others. Tell listeners you want to show them one other way they should not pray. Then show the video clip.

Sister Mary Clarence's prayer is a good example of how *not* to pray. Her prayer is totally insincere. After the clip, discuss how many of our prayers may lack sincerity, just as Sister Mary Clarence's did. Encourage listeners to consider these questions about prayer:

- **What guidelines does Scripture give us on how to pray with sincerity and effectiveness?**
- **Do you pray regularly? Why or why not?**

In your sermon, suggest that listeners strengthen their prayer life by setting aside a certain time of day for prayer and meditation with God. Suggest starting prayer journals to record their prayers and see how God answers them.

....

TiTLE: *Star Trek: Generations* (Paramount Pictures)

THeMe: Time

SCRiPTURe: Ecclesiastes 3: 1-11

Related Passages: Ephesians 5:8-10 and Proverbs 20:7

Overview: Members of the Starship Enterprise are searching through the rubble after the craft crashed, looking for mementos.

Start Time: about 1 hour, 51 minutes into the movie

Start Cue: Commander Riker and Captain Picard are digging through rubble. Reiker pulls out a scrapbook and says, "Is this it?"

End Time: about 1 hour, 52 minutes into the movie

End Cue: Picard says, "After all, we're only mortal."

Comments: Immediately after Picard's comments about being mortal, Riker says, "Speak for yourself; I plan to live forever." Be sure to stop the clip before these words. They don't relate to the point of this sermon starter and could raise many other unrelated and complicated questions in the minds of your listeners.

Application: Bring your calendar or personal planner with you for your sermon. Use it to point out the various activities you've done over the last few months—weddings, funerals, building committee meetings, visiting members in the hospital or a family with a new baby, and so on. Encourage the people in your congregation to think for a minute about recent events in their lives, both good and bad. Then lead into a sermon about how God has a reason for each event in our lives. As you speak, encourage listeners to consider these questions:

- **Why do we avoid thinking about our own mortality?**
- **How could focusing on our mortality actually improve the quality and effectiveness of our lives?**

TITLE: *Stomp Out Loud* (HBO Home Video)

THEME: Self worth

SCRIPTURE: Genesis 5:1-2

Related Passages: 1 Samuel 17:17-31; Exodus 3-4:17; Judges 16:1-22; and 1 Corinthians 12:12-27

Overview: In this video clip, you will see trash and ordinary household objects used to make music. In the same way, God uses ordinary people in extraordinary ways and makes incredible things happen in our lives—even though we may feel quite ordinary.

Start Time: about 5 minutes into the movie

Start Cue: The movie title appears and the camera settles into a city scene.

End Time: about 8 minutes into the movie

End Cue: The music and the frame fade with the players still suspended from the sign.

Comments: The entire video is appropriate for family viewing.

Application: Play the video segment. Emphasize how what people consider being a throwaway was used in this video to actually make music. Have people in the congregation briefly recount success stories of people who overcame great odds to achieve significant success. Then have someone read Genesis 5:1-2. Continue your discussion by asking these questions:

- **How might someone who is struggling with low self-worth be encouraged by this passage? Explain.**
- **How might comparing ourselves with others damage our self-worth?**
- **When we feel ugly, unusable, or unlovable, what can we do to break free from these feelings?**
- **How can we help others who struggle with self-worth?**

TITLE: *Summer of the Monkeys* (Buena Vista Home Video)
THEME: Putting others first
SCRIPTURE: Philippians 2:3-4
Related Passages: Romans 12:3; Ephesians 5:1-2; and Acts 20:35
Overview: A boy in the old west has earned eighty-five dollars with which he desperately wants to buy a pony. Instead, he gives up the money willingly so that his sister can have surgery that will enable her to walk normally.

Start Time: about 1 hour, 34 minutes into the movie
Start Cue: Girl calls out "Grandpa" from a horse.
End Time: about 1 hour, 37 minutes into the movie
End Cue: Boy walks away from the house, holding the horse by the reins.
Comments: The video clip could also be a dramatic ending to a message, leaving people with a powerful illustration of what putting others first really means.

Application: At the beginning of a sermon, this could be a powerful introduction to the topic of selfless living. Consider starting the video without comment and then reading Philippians 2:3-4 before leading into your message. In your sermon, encourage listeners to consider these questions:

- Why is it better to give than to get?
- How does giving sacrificially impact both the recipient and the giver?
- Why should the things you give cost you something?

....

TITLE: *The Truman Show* (Paramount Pictures)

THEME: Free will

SCRIPTURE: Genesis 3

Related Passages: Deuteronomy 30:19-20 and Joshua 24:15

Overview: *The Truman Show* is about a director named Christoff who makes a 24-hours-a-day TV show that records the life of Truman Burbank. Everyone in Truman's life is an actor in the show, his "world" is a giant sound studio, and Christoff contrives many of the events in his life. Sylvia, a former cast member, calls to tell Christoff he is wrong in making a show out of Truman's life because it makes him a prisoner.

Start Time: just over 1 hour, 6 minutes into the movie

Start Cue: The man on the television says, "Sylvia…"

End Time: about 1 hour, 8 minutes into the movie

End Cue: Sylvia hangs up the phone.

Comments: Other parts of this movie contain material that may not be appropriate for family viewing.

Application: Use this clip to begin a sermon about how God gives us free will to choose between right and wrong. Bring a puppet or marionette with you for your sermon. Hold up the puppet and ask the listeners:

- **Does it seem as though we're God's "puppets," with God pulling the strings to control our lives? Why or why not?**

Show the video clip, then ask the listeners to consider these questions:

- **How are we like Truman? How are we different?**
- **If God is all-powerful, why would he give us free will and allow the possibility of making wrong choices?**

TITLE: *The Wizard of Oz* (MGM)

THEME: Integrity

SCRIPTURE: 1 Kings 9:4-5

Related Passages: Proverbs 10:9 and 11:3

Overview: Dorothy and her friends have successfully "melted" the Wicked Witch of the West and have taken her broomstick back to the Wizard of Oz. The wizard had promised to grant their requests if they met this challenge.

Start Time: about 1 hour, 21 minutes into the movie

Start Cue: The wizard asks, "Why have you come back?"

End Time: about 1 hour, 24 minutes into the movie

End Cue: The wizard says that he's a good man, but "a very bad wizard."

Comments: Since most children have seen this movie, seeing the pretend wizard shouldn't scare them. Toto is the scene-stealer here, as he pulls back the curtain to reveal the real wizard.

Application: Show the video clip, then encourage the listeners to consider these questions:

- **Does the wizard have integrity in this movie? Why or why not?**
- **What does a person of integrity look like? How can we recognize him or her?**

Explain that the word "integrity" is mentioned about twenty times in the Bible (NIV version) and is found in Proverbs as well as in association with David and Jesus. David, especially, is held as an example of a man of integrity, specifically by God in 1 Kings 9:4-5. Read the passage, then explain how the Wizard of Oz is a classic example of someone who has little integrity. He doesn't keep his promises, and he is pretending to be someone he's not. Encourage listeners to think of people with integrity whom they admire and discuss why God values integrity so highly. Challenge people to conduct their lives with more integrity as they try to live their lives by Christian principles.

TiTLE: *What Dreams May Come* (Polygram Filmed Entertainment)

THEME: Heaven

SCRiPTURE: John 14:1-4

Related Passages: Mark 16:19; 2 Corinthians 5:8; and 2 Peter 3:13

Overview: Dr. Chris James Nielsen and his wife lost their two children in a car accident four years ago. On his way home one evening, Chris stops to help a person involved in a car accident. The driver of another car loses control and Chris is fatally wounded. The remainder of the film deals with Chris' experience in heaven.

Start Time: just over 32 minutes into the movie

Start Cue: The young speaker says, "Why is it so hard?"

End Time: just over 34 minutes into the movie

End Cue: The two actors take a sip of their coffee and laugh.

Comments: Before this scene, there are several conversations about where the two actors are. You may want to view the scenes before and after the cued scene to get a better idea of the direction of the movie.

Application: During the week before your sermon, gather information from several different religions and philosophies regarding the nature of heaven. Include philosophies such as reincarnation and new age thought. Begin your sermon by explaining what these other philosophies consider heaven to be like. Then show the movie clip to illustrate what many people think about heaven today.

Read John 14:1-4 (and other Scriptures) to help your congregation understand what God says about heaven. Encourage listeners to consider these questions:

- **Why does the Bible speak less about heaven than it does about hell?**
- **What would you like to know about the nature of heaven?**
- **Does the nature of heaven concern you? If so, what are your concerns?**

Section 2:

CREATIVE ACTIVITIES

TiTLE: Open to Interpretation

THEME: The Bible

SCRiPTURE: 2 Timothy 3:16-17

Related Passages: Isaiah 40:8; 2 Timothy 2:15; and Hebrews 4:12

Overview: In this activity, the pastor will show the congregation an abstract painting or sculpture and ask people to interpret its meaning. This opener illustrates the importance of considering all the information available when interpreting the Bible.

Opener: Show your congregation an abstract painting or sculpture. Be sure to use a piece of art that can be interpreted in many different ways.

Ask people to look closely at the artwork, then tell you what they think it represents. Encourage several responses, then say: **The only way to truly understand what the artwork represents is to ask the artist. Without knowing the motivation, circumstances, and process behind the work, we'll all interpret the artwork differently. Interpreting the Bible can be similar.**

Application: Read—or have people in the congregation read—a few Bible passages that sound confusing when one doesn't understand the context. For example, you might want to read passages such as Job 4:7-11; Isaiah 30:1-5; 1 Corinthians 15:29; and James 5:13-15. Then use some Bible study tools to present some information on historical, textual, and cultural context to explain the passages.

Continue your sermon, emphasizing the importance of *studying* the Bible, not just *reading* it.

TiTLE: In Tune

THEME: Christ as our example

SCRiPTURE: 1 Peter 2:21

Related Passages: 1 Corinthians 11:1; Ephesians 5:21; and 1 Timothy 1:16

Overview: Use a pitch pipe or an electronic tuner to fine-tune a guitar, providing an auditory illustration of how Christ's life sets the example for us.

Opener: Loosen the strings on a guitar. Play each of them individually. Acknowledge that some of the congregation may not be aware that the guitar is seriously out of tune. Introduce the pitch pipe or tuner, making sure that its notes can be heard through your microphone system. Then begin to tune each string to the pitch of the tuner. As you tune, talk about how the initial adjustments require a lot of action while making radical adjustments in the tension of each string. Explain how the more adjustment that has been done, the more carefully the tension must be modified. Note how you must again and again return to the tuner to perfect the pitch. Finish tuning one or more strings, and allow the congregation to appreciate the difference.

If a trained guitarist is available, you might want to have him or her play the guitar—first untuned, then tuned—to emphasize the difference your careful attention to the tuning device makes.

Application: Without a tuning device, all we have is a vague idea of how each string of the guitar should sound. In the same way, Christ's example provides us with an objective standard for fine-tuning our spiritual lives. We must constantly evaluate our attitudes and actions in relation to Christ's example. The Holy Spirit enables us to "hear" and makes the adjustments necessary to bring us "in tune" with Christ. Continue your sermon, bringing out different aspects of our lives that must be conformed to Christ's example. As you teach, you may want to ask one or more of the following questions to inspire further thought:

- **What are the "tuning devices" you depend on to understand Christ's example?**
- **What are some important reasons an instrument must be well-tuned? How do those reasons relate to you as an instrument of God?**

....

TITLE: Let's Make a Meal
THEME: Confidence in God
SCRIPTURE: Matthew 7:9-11
Related Passages: Psalm 77:13-14; Proverbs 3:5-6; and Romans 8:28
Overview: In this activity, a volunteer will attempt to discover the real "value meal" to help you illustrate the point that we can have confidence in God's direction.

Opener: You will need two slow cookers. Before church, cook a pot roast or other savory goodie in one of the cookers. Place a restaurant gift certificate inside the other. Put them near the place where you stand to preach. Throw a towel over each of the cookers. If it's feasible to plug in the one with the roast, do so. The smell will pique the congregation's interest. As you begin your sermon, ask for a volunteer who is hungry. Explain that you have prepared two pots for the person to select from, based on his or her hunger. Ask the person to close his or her eyes as you allow a brief exploration of the two pots. You might lift the lids or allow the person to touch or lift the pots or otherwise try to determine which pot has what he or she wants. Try to encourage the person to select the gift certificate in spite of the sensory information he or she gathers. Allow the person to choose, and leave the pots in place until after the sermon.

Application: Point out that both pots contained good things. One was quite obviously a solution to the hunger problem; the other required a bit more faith. Read Matthew 7:9-11. Talk about how when we have needs we bring to God in prayer, he allows us to explore options and gather information. God also advises us in much the same way you advised the volunteer. Sometimes what we hear from God doesn't quite jive with the information we gather. Nevertheless, God's promise is to give good gifts to those who ask. Consider asking one or all of the following questions:

- **When has God given you a gift that felt like an empty pot?**
- **How do you sense God's advice when you are choosing between two good options?**
- **What do you do when you find you have made a mistake?**

TITLE: The People's Language
THEME: Sharing the gospel
SCRIPTURE: 1 Corinthians 9:20
Related Passages: Acts 17:22-31 and 1 Corinthians 14:19

Overview: In this activity, the pastor will create confusion by introducing the sermon with an animated but unintelligible monologue. This attention grabber will set the stage for a sermon about the importance of presenting the gospel using the language of the hearer rather than relying on the passion of the speaker.

Opener: This activity is perfect for the pastor who has a good command of a second language, but if you don't know another actual language, you can achieve the same result by creating your own. For example, write out your script ahead of time, and practice reading it backwards until you are comfortable delivering the words. You will be most effective if you add gestures and use emotional tone and body language.

Application: Before launching into the "real" body of the sermon, ask:

- **What feelings did my opening create for you?**
- **What would you have wanted to do if I had continued the entire sermon in the same way?**
- **How might your experience of the opening of my sermon be similar to the church experience of those who haven't learned "church language"?**

Translate the message you were trying to communicate in the beginning, being sure to note your sincerity, your careful articulation, and the significance of your message. Continue to talk about the biblical basis of becoming all things to all people so that they might, by some means, understand the gospel.

....

TITLE: Little Christs
THEME: Being Christlike
SCRIPTURE: 1 John 4:17
Related Passages: Romans 8:29; 2 Corinthians 3:18; and Philippians 3:10
Overview: In this activity, the pastor will present two items that are identical in every way except size. Participants from the congregation will help the pastor make the point that Christians should have the same description as Christ, by whose name they are called.

Opener: Locate two items that are identical in every way except size. You might find cans of vegetables, stuffed animals, or a key chain-size replica of a larger item. If you can't find any of these examples, you could use an object and a photo of the same thing.

Ask for two volunteers to help you. Have them stand near you, back to back so they can't see each other. Give one the small object and one the larger object. Begin to ask them descriptive questions, such as "What color is the nose of your object?" Continue until each volunteer has answered several questions identically. Finally, ask if they believe they are holding the same items. Have them show each other the items, and ask them to identify the differences. Thank the participants and have them be seated.

Application: Use this illustration to launch a sermon about our representation of Christ. Remind your congregation that the word Christian means "little Christ." You might consider asking the following questions:

- **Why is it important that we be conformed to the image of Christ?**
- **How are you like Christ? How are you different?**

TITLE: What Are You Waiting For?
THEME: Waiting for God
SCRIPTURE: Psalm 130:6
Related Passages: Psalms 27:14; 37:34; and 38:15
Overview: In this activity, the pastor will instill an atmosphere of discomfort by not following the anticipated rhythm of the service to make the point that waiting for the Lord can be uncomfortable but sometimes necessary.

Opener: Begin the service in your customary manner. When it's time for the sermon, remain seated. Listen carefully for the sounds your silence inspires. These sounds can be noted later as evidence of discomfort. Wait until someone asks about your purpose or until you sense that the congregation has resigned itself to your silence. It's even possible that the Holy Spirit will begin to speak to individuals as you wait. Be sensitive to his movement.

When you stand to speak, break the silence by reading the words of your selected Scriptures. Let them speak for themselves. Depending on the mood, you may choose to wait a few moments longer before delivering your message.

Application: Begin by discussing the mood of waiting you just experienced together and the course the mood followed. Point out the sounds and feelings you perceived as you waited together. You can ask for the congregation's input about their perceptions of the delay. You may wish to ask one or all of the following questions:

- **When have you had to wait for the Lord? How did it feel? How was it like or unlike what we just experienced together?**
- **What is your typical response to having to wait?**
- **What are some positive outcomes you believe God wants you to experience as a result of waiting? How can you focus on those outcomes as you are in the midst of waiting?**

TITLE: Peace Blessing
THEME: Peace
SCRIPTURE: John 14:27

Related Passages: Romans 5:1; Philippians 4:6-7; and 1 Thessalonians 5:13

Overview: This activity provides opportunity for all worshipping to be blessed by God's peace and to pass that peace on to each other.

Activity: At close of the worship time, begin singing a song about God's peace. During the singing, reach out and touch another person on the shoulder, and have him or her then touch another person, so that a "domino effect" occurs. Instruct everyone to keep their hands on others' shoulders so that everyone is eventually touching and being touched.

Application: Ask the listeners for input about the impact of touching and being touched. You may wish to ask one or all of the following questions:

- **When have you needed God's peace and found it? How was it like or unlike what we just experienced together?**
- **What is your typical reaction to stress or worry?**
- **What are some positive outcomes you believe God wants you to experience as a result of walking in his peace? How can you focus on his peace in the midst of stressful situations?**

TITLE: Love Can Be Messy
THEME: Loving others
SCRIPTURE: 1 Corinthians 13:4-7

Related Passages: Matthew 5:44; John 15:13; and Ephesians 4:2

Overview: This activity will use candy to provide a visual reminder of the difficulties of loving with persistence.

Opener: You'll need a damp cloth for this messy activity. Ask three volunteers to help you. Give one an unwrapped chocolate candy bar, one a roll of hard candies, and one several pieces of licorice. Say that you are giving each of your assistants something you hope he or she will love. These different kinds of candy represent different kinds of people God wants us to love. Tell them you want them to get really close to their assignment—by unwrapping the treats and holding them tightly in their hands. Talk about the feelings we might experience as we enter into a ministry of love, whether it's with a spouse, a child, a fellow Christian, or an enemy. We anticipate the sweetness of the relationship because the God we trust has given the assignment.

You'll want to elaborate on this until you're certain the chocolate is beginning to melt in your assistant's hands. Then have each person open his or her hands to show the results of carrying out your request. Talk about how it doesn't take long for us to begin to notice that relationships can get sticky and that some can have some pretty messy consequences. Thank your assistants by giving each a wrapped version of the candy you originally asked them to hold. Let them wipe their hands and be seated.

Application: Note that you could have let each assistant simply have the candy you had originally given him or her to hold. For one or two of them, that might have been a reward in and of itself. For the person holding the chocolate, it probably wouldn't have been appreciated. Instead the reward came not from the candy itself but from obedience to your request to hold the candy. Too often, we expect a reward to come from the loving relationship God has entrusted to us. Instead, God rewards obedience to his command to love, even when the act of persistent loving becomes messy or unpleasant.

As you continue your sermon, you may wish to ask one or all of the following questions:

- **Who are the "chocolate people" in your life?**
- **What has God taught you through enduring love?**
- **How do you feel about putting emphasis on obedience to God's command to love patiently instead of on the love relationship itself?**

....

TITLE: Mirror, Mirror

THEME: How God sees us

SCRIPTURE: Psalm 51:6

Related Passages: Job 7:17-18 and Psalm 139:1

Overview: Use mirrors to help people relate a visual image to the way the Holy Spirit reveals to us our inmost thoughts as we allow him to.

Opener: Display a variety of types of mirrors at the entrance to your worship area. Make sure the display is right in the line of traffic so that it's difficult to avoid. Your display could include a hand mirror, a magnifying mirror, and a full-length mirror. You may wish to add a sign that says, "Take a look."

Application: Begin by asking what some of the thoughts were upon encountering the mirrors at the entrance to the sanctuary. Say: **Part of the worship experience is reflection. We reflect on what God has done and is doing. But as we do that, he also gives us the opportunity to see ourselves as he sees us. He desires "truth in the inner parts."** Talk about how some of us avoid God's intent to show us the inmost parts, just as some of them chose to avoid the mirrors. Some of us avoid giving God our full attention for fear of what he might show us. When we keep those defenses up, we never see ourselves as we truly are. Some of us come to God determined to allow only one small area of our lives to be brought under his authority. We choose to see that one area with the intensity of the magnifying mirror, but we neglect the rest of our lives. Some of us come asking God to help us "see it all" in the full-length mirror. Continue the sermon, challenging people to pursue the honest image that only God can offer. You may want to ask one or all of the following questions.

- **What keeps you from seeing yourself as God sees you?**
- **What things need to be cleared away from your life to get to "truth in the inmost parts"?**
- **How do you think or fear your life might change by allowing God to illuminate every part?**

....

TITLE: Cut Flowers
THEME: Staying connected to Jesus
SCRIPTURE: John 15:5
Related Passages: 1 Samuel 16:7 and Matthew 7:19 and 23:27
Overview: The congregation will examine cut carnations to help them think about what happens to a plant separated from its life source, much as Jesus detailed in the passage about the vine and the branches.

Opener: Plan to have one cut carnation for each row in your worship area. Try to obtain carnations that have unopened buds on each stem. Arrange them in a large container with floral foam at the bottom to help each flower stand. If you have a large congregation, use only a portion of the stems in the arrangement, and supply the ushers with the remainder. (Feel free to enlist the help of a florist in creating a full arrangement.) Begin by pointing out the beauty of the arrangement. Give attention to detail. Then start pulling the carnations out of the arrangement. Say: **As beautiful as these flowers are, they are horribly flawed. I'd like you to look at them and see if you can detect some of their problems.** Begin to pass the flowers to the congregation, one to each row. Have them pass the flower around and discuss its limitations with the person sitting next to them.

Application: If you have made this a small-group activity, ask the congregation for feedback on their group's discussion. If you haven't, point out some or all of the following problems.
- When the flower was attached to the plant, it stood tall. Now it falls.
- The appearance is deceptive. While the flower looks healthy, it is, in fact, doomed.

- The flower is no longer receiving nutrients from the plant. It's dying and the
  buds will not reach their potential, nor will any more buds be produced.

  Use the flower to draw parallels to John 15:5 throughout your sermon. Allow the youngest (or oldest) member of each row to take the carnation home.

TITLE: A Squiggle in Eternity
THEME: Body of Christ
SCRIPTURE: Ephesians 4:1
Related Passages: 1 Corinthians 12:7 and Hebrews 12:1
Overview: In this activity, members of the congregation will help you illustrate the impact of one person's contribution to the body of Christ by turning the projected image of a meaningless squiggle into a meaningful message.

Opener: Set up an overhead projector and screen. Draw a free-form squiggle on a transparency. Choose five people to help you with this active illustration. Tell your volunteers you'd like each of them to add one detail to the squiggle that will transform it into what they imagine it will be in the end. They may add anything that helps to bring meaning to the developing picture. Hand the first person a transparency pen, and watch what develops.

Application: Before launching into the body of the sermon, encourage listeners to consider these questions:

- **How does the final picture compare to what you initially imagined when you saw the squiggle?**
- **What changed your perspective?**
- **How is this picture like what happens in the body of Christ as each person makes a contribution?**

As you continue the message, discuss how the church today builds upon what the "great cloud of witnesses" has contributed before us. What we leave behind will dramatically impact what the church becomes tomorrow.

TITLE: Worm Theology

THEME: God's plans

SCRIPTURE: Job 25:6

Related Passages: Psalm 8:4; Isaiah 55:9; and 2 Corinthians 4:7

Overview: Use worms to stimulate reflection on God's great plan for humanity.

Opener: Before church, obtain a supply of night crawlers from a bait store (or harvest your own). Place them in a small container so they are easy to find. Read the words to Isaac Watts' hymn "Alas and Did My Savior Bleed?"

Alas! and did my Savior bleed

And did my Sovereign die?

Would He devote that sacred head

For such a worm as I?

Pick up one of the worms and walk through the congregation. Allow people to respond uniquely to this living analogy. Be sensitive to those who do not want to get near it.

Application: Watts' hymn was almost certainly based on Job 25:6. Many modern hymnals have changed the original text because the analogy of the worm is offensive to many and reeks of "poor self-image."

Ask the congregation to think about all the things they can do that the worm cannot. The gap between our abilities and God's abilities is surely even greater; yet God has chosen to use people as vehicles for bringing his message to the world.

Share these facts about worms:

- Earthworms nourish growing plants. They break up the soil and mix it, causing important plant nutrients to become distributed throughout the soil. As we move through the world, we "mix" in touches of God's grace, preparing the soil for God's work of redemption.

- Earthworms come in many shapes and sizes ranging from $1/25$ of an inch to eleven feet long. Christians, too, look different from each other and have specialized ministries; yet we all have the job of keeping the soil prepared.

• An earthworm moves by stretching forward, then bringing the rest of its body along. We, too, must reach forward in faith, often out of our comfort zones, and bring the rest of ourselves along after faith has made a way.

Certainly the role God has entrusted to us shows the immense value God places on us who are created in his image. Still the comparison of our abilities to the worm's and God's abilities to ours helps us to feel awed by God's mighty power.

TITLE: A Ton of Bricks
THEME: Doctrine
SCRIPTURE: Matthew 7:24

Related Passages: Titus 1:9 and 2:1 and 2 Timothy 2:15

Overview: In this activity, you will use a sack of bricks to illustrate how sound doctrine forms a foundation for faith.

Opener: Fill a pillowcase with bricks. Carry it with you as you stand to preach. You can either ask for several volunteers to each come and hold a brick and tell something he or she could do with it, or you can pull out one brick at a time and highlight a purpose for each. For example, you might tell one person to practice using it as a weapon or to stand on it to appear taller.

Application: Bricks are versatile tools. You can carry them around as you did when you brought them to your worship service. You can throw them. You can build walls with them. You can use them to build a solid foundation. (Include the observations of any volunteers you used.)

The doctrines of the church can be used in the same ways. You can carry them around like a heavy burden to show people how spiritual you are. You can throw them as weapons, telling people how they should live or how they "just don't measure up." You can use doctrines to build a wall of exclusion, telling people that that they must believe exactly as you do on everything (including nonessentials) or they can't be a part of your church. Or you can use them to build a firm foundation for a loving life of service that will draw others to Christ.

You may wish to ask one or all of the following questions:

- **What's the difference between using a doctrine to correct and teach and using a doctrine as a weapon?**
- **How have you seen doctrines divide people?**
- **How have you seen doctrines protect people?**

Continue your sermon, highlighting some specific basic doctrines that unite Christians. You might consider giving each worshipper a brick to record these doctrines as a reminder of your message.

TiTLE: Sweet Service

THEME: Serving God

SCRIPTURE: Philippians 2:3

Related Passages: Matthew 6:24 and 16:5 and John 6:44

Overview: Use various candy bars to examine some of the reasons for serving God.

Opener: You will need a Payday, a $100,000 Bar, a Mr. Goodbar, a Snickers, and Dove chocolates (one Dove per person, if possible). Place all of them except the Dove chocolates in a brown bag. Tell the worshippers that each item in the bag represents a reason people have for following God. Ask four people to select from the bag one at a time.

As the candy bars are drawn out, make the following interpretations:

- PayDay—Some people are motivated by the desire to gain the reward of heaven.
- $100,000 candy bar—Some people are motivated by a desire for prosperity in this life. The prosperity-seeker may be seeking emotional rather than financial gain.
- Mr. Goodbar—Some people are motivated by the desire to be good and moral.
- Snickers—Some people are motivated to serve God for the fun or exhilaration of it.

Application: All of these candy bars represent some result of serving God. None of the things mentioned are wrong in and of themselves. God does promise eternal life. He also promises abundant life, which sometimes translates into emotional or financial prosperity. God helps us live morally upright lives. He also offers wonderful times of fun through an emotional response to a spiritual event. These things, however, cannot be our reasons for serving God because his Word tells us to do nothing out of selfish ambition. Instead, our motivation must come from the prompting of the Holy Spirit, which is represented in your analogy by the Dove chocolates. Share these with your worshippers. Continue your teaching on the importance of the right motivation for service.

As you teach, encourage listeners to consider these questions:

- **How does maturity impact our motivation to serve?**
- **How can you tell if you are improperly motivated?**
- **What is your response when the "payoffs" of service seem too far removed from your daily life?**

TITLE: Wake Up
THEME: Impacting the world
SCRIPTURE: 2 Corinthians 5:20
Related Passages: Matthew 5:13 and 13:33 and John 7:34
Overview: Use a wind-up alarm clock to add emphasis to some of the community or world concerns that call Christians to action.

Opener: Select issues from the local, regional, or national news that have alarming potential consequences. Become familiar with your wind-up alarm clock ahead of time so that you know how many concerns you can highlight. Synchronize the alarm and the time just prior to your sermon so that you can turn the ringer on and off. Before you start listing concerns, turn on the ringer so that the alarm sounds. Then list the news articles. As you read, you can either use the words "I'm alarmed that…" or "Wake up" to add emphasis to the news story.

Application: Use these stories as a call to become actively involved as an ambassador of Christ in the complex world in which we live. Challenge your congregation to think seriously about their roles as ambassadors of Christ. You may wish to ask one or more of the following questions:

- **Which of these concerns touch your heart most deeply?**

• **Which Bible passages speak directly to this issue?**

• **If you were to truly "wake up" about this issue, what would you do?**

Remember as you preach that it is far more important to help your worshippers seek God's direction in responding to their world than to tell them what their responses should or should not be.

....

TiTLe: The Value of a Woman

THeMe: Women

SCRiPTURe: Proverbs 31:30-31

Related Passages: 1 Timothy 5:1b-2 and Titus 2:3-4

Overview: This activity provides an opportunity to honor women without creating awkwardness for those who are childless. It can be done at any point in the worship service. For this activity, you'll need a small table, centrally located and covered with a quilt; a crocheted doily; a hat box; an antique brooch; old photos of women; or similar items. Also have an empty basket on the table. Give a blank sheet of paper to each person as he or she enters worship.

Opener: The writer of Proverbs knows that "a woman who fears the Lord is to be praised." This activity provides an opportunity for that praise.

Application: Invite listeners to recall a woman who made a difference in their lives and write her name on the paper you provided. Ask two or three people in the congregation to share about the women they chose. Then invite all the participants to come forward, placing their papers in the basket. (Be sure to assist anyone who cannot come forward easily.)

After all the papers are in the basket, share the following prayer: **Dear God, we praise you for each woman remembered here today. We thank you for the gift of womanhood and for the nurture that has touched our lives. We praise you for memories so fondly cherished. As we honor the gifts of women, may we celebrate the glory you have revealed through all of your daughters. Amen.**

TITLE: He Said, She Said

THEME: Doubting God

SCRIPTURE: Psalm 145:13

Related Passages: Proverbs 3:5; John 14:1; and Psalm 146:6

Overview: In this activity, the pastor will compare the emotions felt when we doubt friends and then ask for their forgiveness with the emotions we should feel when we doubt God.

Opener: Before your sermon, arrange for a volunteer to interrupt you as you begin to speak. The volunteer will break in and say that he or she simply must discuss a pressing personal problem with you.

Have the volunteer relate a tale of a seemingly broken friendship as you try to break into the monologue to offer counsel. The conversation might go something like this:

Volunteer: **I'm so sorry to interrupt you like this, but I really need to talk to you. It's about Mary. You know Mary—my *so-called* best friend.**

You: **Yes, I was just talking to Mary, and…**

Volunteer: **Well, every week she calls and asks if I need a ride to church because you know how unreliable my car can be. I can usually count on her, but this week—*this* week of all weeks—she didn't call.**

You: **Yes, well, that's because…**

Volunteer: **She *knew* how important today was to me. Today's the day I'm to present the Sunday school program for the whole year to all the new teachers, and I really needed to be here early.**

You: **But the reason she didn't call is that…**

Volunteer: **Don't bother. The reason she didn't call is that she doesn't care about me, that's all. I thought you should know how utterly unreliable she is and how she treats people who put their trust in her.**

You: **What I'm trying to tell you is that Mary didn't call to offer you a ride this morning because she needed to be here early herself. You'll see why after the service…I guess I might as well tell you, although it was to**

be a surprise. Mary planned a special reception for you to recognize your hard work with the Sunday school. It was all her idea, and she did all the arranging and baking. I'm surprised you would ever doubt her after all these years!

Application: Ask your listeners to suppose what your volunteer will now say and think about Mary. Then have them think of times they have doubted friends or loved ones, just as your volunteer did. How did they feel? What did they do?

Continue your sermon, drawing parallels between how easily we misjudge and doubt those we care about on earth and how often and easily we doubt God's love. Emphasize that just as we feel remorse when we misjudge friends, we should feel remorse for doubting God, who loves us more completely than any friend ever will. And just as we ask our friends for their forgiveness, we should also come before God with contrite hearts.

TITLE: Keeping First Things First
THEME: Priorities
SCRIPTURE: Luke 10:38-42
Related Passages: Philippians 3:4-16 and Matthew 7:24-27

Overview: In this activity, participants will try to keep several balloons aloft at once to illustrate the difficulty in keeping our priorities in order. For this activity, you'll need three round balloons for each participant (one blue balloon and two white ones). You'll also need markers.

Opener: Distribute the balloons and markers (one blue balloon and two whites to each participant). Have participants inflate and tie their balloons. Then have each person write on the blue balloon his or her first priority in life. Then on the white balloons, have participants write their second and third priorities, each on a separate balloon.

At your signal, have participants bounce their blue balloons into the air with their hands, trying not to allow the balloons to hit the floor. As they do this, talk about the importance of keeping first things first and staying focused on what's most important in life.

Then, while still bouncing the blue balloons, have participants begin bouncing the white balloons on which they wrote their second priority. As participants continue to bounce both balloons, talk about how even good but less important priorities can distract us from what's most important.

Finally, have participants add the final balloon to their bouncing efforts. At this point, most will have great difficulty keeping any of their balloons aloft. Talk to participants about what can happen in our lives if we let our priorities get out of order: Very soon, none of our priorities will be priorities, giving way instead to the tyranny of the urgent and a stressed-out, unfocused life.

Close by having participants write on their balloons some specific things that sometimes distract them from keeping the priority in its proper order in their lives. They can either keep these balloons as a reminder of their priorities and the importance of keeping them in proper order or pop them after you lead them in a prayer of dedication of their lives and priorities to God.

Application: This activity can be used to make a point about priorities, becoming overly committed, staying devoted to Christ, living a balanced life, and many other issues. As you explore these issues, you might want to encourage listeners to consider these questions:

  • **How did it feel to try to balance all three balloons at once?**
  • **How is that like how it feels to balance your priorities in real life?**
  • **What can we do as Christians to help us keep our priorities in order?**

TITLE: Not Interested!

THEME: Temptation

SCRIPTURE: 1 Corinthians 10:13

Related Passages: Matthew 26:41 and James 4:7

Overview: In this activity, the pastor will receive several sales calls at the beginning of the sermon. This opener compares annoying calls to temptations.

Opener: Before the sermon, arrange for a helper to make several calls to you as you begin to speak. If possible, have a speakerphone set up near the pulpit. If a speakerphone isn't feasible, use a cellular phone and ad lib the dialogue.

Begin the sermon by saying that you have something very important about God to tell the congregation. As you begin the sermon, your helper should make a series of annoying sales calls to you. (You know—the kind of calls that always come during dinner!) For example, your helper might offer you a free vacation, a new mortgage at a lower interest rate, cheaper phone service, or siding for your house.

During each conversation, tell the caller that you're busy and that you're not interested in what he or she is selling. Then hang up.

Application: Use this demonstration to compare the annoying sales calls you received to the temptations that Satan constantly throws our way. Challenge people to feel as justified in resisting temptations as they do in ignoring unwanted sales pitches. Point out that just as focusing on the calls kept you from delivering your sermon, temptations can keep us from accomplishing the good works God has planned for us.

TITLE: The Great Commission
THEME: Sharing faith
SCRIPTURE: Matthew 28:19-20
Related Passages: Romans 15:20 and Acts 10:42-43
Overview: In this activity, several red roses will be passed from the back of the sanctuary to the pulpit. This opener will stress the importance of spreading the good news about Jesus.

Opener: Begin your sermon by explaining that you have some very important objects that need to be passed from the back of the sanctuary to the front. Have helpers distribute several red roses to those sitting in the rear of the room, and ask people to pass the roses forward. If possible, use roses that have many thorns. That will strengthen the illustration.

When the roses have been passed to the front row, ask that they be brought forward to you.

Application: Explain that passing the roses in this activity is like telling others about Jesus. Challenge people to think about these questions:

- **What was it like to be one of the people passing the roses?**

- **Were the roses easy to pass? Why or why not?**

- **What was it like never to have a rose passed to you?**

- **What would happen if people simply refused to pass the roses?**

Continue your sermon, challenging your listeners to be willing to pass the good news of Jesus on to those who might never otherwise hear of him.

....

TiTLE: Grow Up!

THEME: Growing in faith

SCRIPTURE: 1 Corinthians 13:11-12

Related Passages: Mark 10:15; Ephesians 4:15; and 2 Peter 3:18

Overview: In this opener, the pastor will demonstrate that children learn more and become more accomplished as they grow older. The activity will highlight the fact that no matter how much we think we know about God, we're all still learning and growing in our faith.

Opener: Before this activity, arrange to have several children brought forward at the start of the sermon. You'll want an infant, a toddler, a younger elementary child, and an older elementary child.

The object of this opener is to show varying stages of development, understanding, and ability. You can make this activity as simple or as involved as you wish. For an easy demonstration, you might ask each child to do something that requires a higher degree of ability than the preceding child. For example, you could ask the baby to hold a ball. Of course, the baby won't be able to do it. But the toddler will be able to hold the ball and even bounce it. Then the early-elementary child can bounce the ball and clap two times before catching it. Then the oldest child can demonstrate some fancy soccer footwork with the ball. After the demonstration, thank your volunteers and have them sit down. Ask the congregation whether it makes them feel angry or frustrated that the children are at various stages of ball-handling ability.

Application: Use this opener to show that we're all at different levels of Christian growth. Some are still babies in faith, while others appear to have progressed much further in their spiritual development. But to God, we all must seem like young children in our understanding of him. Encourage your listeners to bear with one another in Christian love, no matter what stage of faith their companions may have reached. Challenge your audience to keep their focus on Jesus and to let our loving Lord lead and teach each of us what he wants us to know, in his own good time.

....

TITLE: Lighten Up
THEME: Purity before God
SCRIPTURE: 1 Peter 2:9
Related Passages: Matthew 5:16; 2 Corinthians 4:6; and 1 John 1:7,10
Overview: In this opener, the pastor will use a flashlight to demonstrate that God can see every part of our lives.

Opener: As you begin your sermon, have a helper turn down the lights in the room. If the room has a lot of natural light, you might consider covering the windows before the worship service.

Bring out a flashlight, and turn it on. (The bigger the beam, the better.) Say: **With the lights so dim, it's hard to see deeply into the corners of the room, isn't it? There could be all kinds of creepy things there. There could be cobwebs and spiders and dust and even trash. But since it's so dark, we might assume that no one will ever know what's happening in those corners. But watch what happens when I shine this flashlight into the corner.**

Shine the light into one corner of the room. Say: **Now look—everything in that corner is in clear view. What was hidden is now illuminated by the light.** (For extra impact, hide several signs in the corners of the room before this activity. The signs could say "deceit," "lies," "envy," or "anger.") Repeat the process, shining your light into all the dark recesses of the room.

Application: Compare shining your light into the dark corners of the room to how God can see into the dark corners of our lives. Nothing is hidden from God—he knows our every thought and deed. (And amazingly—he still loves us!)

Challenge your listeners to live lives pleasing to God. Explain that God already knows what's hidden in our dark recesses, and he wants to help us clean up our lives. Encourage people to confess their sins to God and to let him shine his light of forgiveness into the darkest corners of their lives

....

TITLE: No Pain, No Gain
THEME: Perseverance
SCRIPTURE: James 1:2-4
Related Passages: Romans 5:3-4; Hebrews 12:1; and 2 Peter 1:5-6
Overview: In this activity, participants will physically experience perseverance and be rewarded for enduring. You'll need a candy bar prize for each volunteer.

Opener: Select a number of able-bodied volunteers from the congregation. Have them gather at the front of the sanctuary and stand facing the congregation.

Have volunteers each move at least an arm's length from their neighbors. Have participants fully extend their arms from their sides in the shape of a cross. Tell folks to hold their arms in place until you say time is up. If anyone drops or bends their arms, they are out and should sit down. Let volunteers know that those who endure will receive a special surprise!

For four to five minutes (if necessary), continue your message. (To shorten this activity, have participants pick up books in either hand as they hold their arms outstretched. They will tire sooner that way.) You can speak about perseverance, read Scriptures that have to do with endurance, or tell a story of a time when you had to persevere through a difficult time. Of course, realize that everyone will be distracted a bit from what you say. After the activity is completed, repeat anything you feel is vital.

When you are down to one person with arms still extended or time is up, reward persevering participants with a candy bar.

Application: Use this activity to physically illustrate in a fun, simple way what perseverance "feels" like. Perseverance involves enduring a trial or test to gain a benefit or reward of some kind. In this activity, people were willing to endure pain for four or five minutes just for a candy bar, yet few of us are willing to persevere through trials, tests, or hardships to gain a much more valuable prize—

the character of Christ. Too often we respond to tests, trials, and hardships with short tempers, anxiety, fear, or self-pity. These things only cause us to become depressed, stressed, or bitter. When we persevere and face trials and hardships with trust in God and a positive attitude, we will become more like Christ through the experience.

TiTLe: The Old Ball and Chain
THeMe: Freedom from sin
SCRiPTURe: John 8:31-36

Related Passages: Psalm 146:7; Romans 6:18; and Galatians 5:1

Overview: You'll come out with a ball and chain, representing sin, padlocked to your leg. You'll have a variety of keys, only one of which will fit the padlock attaching the chain to your leg. People will try various keys, but only one will unlock the lock—the one labeled "Faith in Jesus."

Opener: Before your message, prepare a ball and chain by painting an old basketball or volleyball black. Then attach it (duct tape works fine) to a chain at least three to four feet long. You'll also need a padlock with a key and at least three extra keys that don't fit the padlock. On the real padlock key, attach a tag that says, "Faith in Jesus." On the other keys, attach tags with messages like "Being a good person," "Doing things for the poor," "Attending church regularly," "Knowing a lot about the Bible," "Giving God lots of money," and "Working for the church."

When you enter for your sermon, have the ball and chain padlocked to your leg, and make it obvious that you are dragging this heavy ball behind you. Comment on how tough it is being chained to this heavy weight of sin. Then say: **I have some keys here. Who would like to come up and try to free me from my sin?**

Have volunteers come up and—one at a time—give them each a key to try. Have each person read the tag on his or her key before trying it. Be sure the correct padlock key is last. When you're freed from the ball and chain, jump and cheer over your freedom.

Application: Thank your volunteers, and use the following questions to lead into your message:

- **How was that ball and chain like the sin in our lives?**
- **What kinds of things do we sometimes do to try to get rid of the guilt caused by that sin?**
- **How does faith in Jesus set us free?**

Move into your message, emphasizing that in Christ we are set free from sin and from the guilt our sins produce.

TITLE: Time for God?
THEME: Spending time with God
SCRIPTURE: Mark 1:35
Related Passages: Luke 6:12; Ephesians 6:18; and 1 Thessalonians 5:17

Overview: To set the stage for your message on the importance of spending time with God, you'll do a little dialog with your spouse, indicating a meager amount of time spent together this past week. Then you'll explain that your dialog was not based on fact but was done to make a point.

Opener: Arrange in advance to do this dialog with your spouse before beginning your message. If you're not married or if your spouse would rather not participate, find a couple who are willing to perform the dialog for the congregation. The couple doesn't have to pretend to be the pastor and spouse—the dialog will work for any married couple.

Pastor: (to spouse) **I need to apologize for spending only about ten minutes with you this week.**

Spouse: **That's all right. You know I love you anyway.**

Pastor: **I know it's not all right, but I get so busy with church work and** [name several other activities you're involved in]. **I just can't fit everything in and still have time for you.**

Spouse: **Well, I forgive you. Do you think we can spend a little more time together this week?**

Pastor: **Sure. I mean, really I love you and all. I hope I can manage to** spend at least five minutes with you every day this week—except for my day off, of course.

Spouse: **If that's all you can manage, I guess I'll have to live with it. I'll be around when you're ready.**

Pastor: **Thanks. I really love you a lot.**

Application: Immediately after this dialog, say: **I've really spent more time than that with my spouse this week, but we did that little dialog to get you thinking about the importance of spending time with someone we truly love.** Then encourage your congregation to consider the following questions:

- **How strong can a love relationship be if two people spend only ten minutes together each week?**
- **How much love is demonstrated by squeezing in only five minutes a day with the one you love?**
- **What parallels do you see between our dialog and the average churchgoer's relationship with God?**

TITLE: Closer to God

THEME: Pleasing God

SCRIPTURE: 2 Corinthians 5:7-9

Related Passages: Psalm 145:17-20; James 4:7-10; and 1 John 5:1-5

Overview: People will throw wads of paper at a target, illustrating how the closer you are to the target, the easier it is to hit. They will then discover how this principle applies to hitting the target of pleasing God in real life.

Opener: Before your message, find, make, or purchase a big target. (A dartboard would do, but bigger would be better.) Prepare in advance for each person in the congregation to have a sheet of paper with "My attempt to please God" written on it. You could put the papers in your bulletin or have them on the seats.

As you begin your message, have everyone get their sheets of paper and wad them into tight balls. Then stand within a few feet of the front row, hold up the target, and say: **This target represents our goal of pleasing God in all we do. Now we're going to see who can hit the bull's-eye.** Begin with the back row, and have everyone stand up and attempt to hit the bull's-eye on your target without moving from their row. Proceed row by row toward the front until all have thrown their papers.

Application: Use the following questions to help your people understand the significance of this activity:

- **Who was able to hit the bull's-eye most easily?**
- **Who didn't stand a chance of hitting it?**
- **How was being closer to the target in this activity like being closer to God in real life?**
- **How can we increase the possibility that we'll be able to live lives pleasing to God?**
- **How can we draw nearer to God in our own lives?**

TITLE: Hungry for Righteousness

THEME: Spiritual hunger

SCRIPTURE: Matthew 5:6

Related Passages: John 6:35, 47-58

Overview: In this activity, the pastor will eat some fragrant food in front of the congregation. This opener sets the stage for a sermon about spiritual hunger.

Opener: When you're preparing to give your sermon, bring with you some fragrant food, such as popcorn or brownies. As you're about to begin your sermon, say: **Before I begin, please excuse me as I eat a little something. This has been such a hectic day, I didn't have a chance to eat anything until now.**

Spend several seconds eating some food in front of the congregation. Watch for their reactions, particularly if they appear to want some of the food themselves! As you eat, you may want to comment on specific people's reactions, such as pointing out other people who look hungry, too.

After several seconds, put away the food and thank the congregation for being patient during your snack.

Application: You can use this illustration to begin a discussion of spiritual hunger. You may want to ask such questions as these:

- **How did you react when I began to eat in front of you?**
- **How did the sight or smell of my food affect you?**
- **How would you describe hunger?**
- **How would you describe spiritual hunger?**

Continue with your sermon, highlighting the parallels between physical hunger and spiritual hunger. Point to Jesus as the source of satisfaction for our spiritual hunger, which we often try to fulfill in other ways.

....

TITLE: Salty Saints
THEME: Impacting the world
SCRIPTURE: Matthew 5:13-16

Related Passages: Mark 9:50; Luke 14:34-35; and Colossians 4:6

Overview: This activity provides an object lesson that participants can take with them wherever they go. It's a reminder that we as Christians are the "salt" of love and justice in the world and that we must not lose our "saltiness." For this activity, you'll need many small packets of salt, such as those found at fast food restaurants. These can be purchased in a large quantity from a wholesale grocery.

Opener: After reading Matthew 5:13-16, tell participants you want them to get a firsthand taste for what Jesus was talking about in this passage.

Have volunteers distribute packets of salt to each row. As participants pass the salt packets along, have them say, "You are the salt of the earth." Once everyone has a packet, have participants tear open a small corner on the packet and taste the salt. If possible, have participants form pairs to discuss how salt is used in everyday life and what those uses can teach us about being the "salt of the earth."

Application: In the Sermon on the Mount, Jesus challenged his followers with the importance of our witness in the world. He anticipated our often lackadaisical approach to the gospel and reminded us that our worth is in our saltiness (Matthew 5:13). As you guide participants to understand what it means to be the "salt of the earth," you might encourage them to consider these questions:

- **In what way are you an "extremely salty" Christian?**

- In what ways have you lost some of your saltiness?
- What can you do this week to make sure you don't lose your "saltiness" in the world?

TiTLe: Wall of Thankfulness
THeMe: Being thankful
SCRiPTURe: Psalm 100:4-5
Related Passages: Philippians 4:6 and Colossians 2:6-7
Overview: In this activity, participants will write notes of thanks to God on a huge "wall" as an extravagant "thanksgiving" offering to God. This activity would work well during the Thanksgiving season.

Opener: Before the service, ask some people in the congregation with a talent for working with wood to create one or more large free-standing partitions (8x8 feet or 6x6 feet will work fine.) You'll need a separate partition or "wall" for every 100 to 150 people in your church service. Cover the front of each wall with white paper.

During the offering time or at the beginning of a communion service, have members of the congregation come forward and write notes of thanksgiving to God on the "wall." At the close of the offering or just before you take communion, read excerpts from the wall before closing with a prayer of thanksgiving to God for his goodness and faithfulness.

Keep the wall on display in the front foyer of the church for at least several weeks as a reminder to the congregation of God's goodness and faithfulness to them.

Application: This activity will give your congregation an opportunity to worship the Lord by giving thanks for all he has done in their lives. It will provide participants with a dramatic reminder of how good God has been and the wonderful things he has done. For as long as you keep the wall displayed, people will be reminded of God's goodness and faithfulness in your church.

TITLE: No Fear!

THEME: Overcoming fear

SCRIPTURE: Psalm 34:4

Related Passages: 2 Timothy 1:6-7 and 1 Peter 3:12-14

Overview: In this activity, participants will inflate or deflate balloons as certain words are read in a story. You'll need a 9-inch balloon for each person.

Opener: Have volunteers distribute balloons to each member of the congregation. When everyone has a balloon, tell the congregation that you are going to begin today's message with something a little different. Say: **I'm about to read a short story. As I read the story, I want you to blow a full breath of air *into* your balloon every time you hear *negative* words like "fear," "death," "afraid," "worry," anxious," and so on. Every time you hear *positive* words like "God," "peace," "faith," "Jesus," and the like, you should let one breath of air *out* of your balloons. Don't worry. I'll cue you as we go through the story.**

Read a few of the key words, and allow everyone to practice to be sure they understand what they are to do. Then begin the activity by reading the following story aloud:

A Fear Story

(You may substitute any name for John in the story if you wish.)

John was not known to be a **fearful** person or one with **anxiety** or **sadness** over his life's circumstances. He certainly never thought of himself as a **fearful** person. He was a good person with a good life. He was a **bold** go-getter and he loved **God**.

One day John was taking a good look at his life and realized the many **fears** that actually were in his life. He **feared** he would someday **lose** his sharpness and **fail** in his career. He was **anxious** that he would not have the money he needed to give his family the best quality of life. He **feared** he was being overlooked in some social circles because he didn't make a higher income. He **feared** his house was not impressive enough, and he **feared** his neighborhood property values might be stifled by recent development nearby. He felt suddenly **anxious** as to whether those closest to him respected him.

At first John decided he would just **pray** to **God** and ask him to **bless** him financially to bring all these good things to his life that he wanted and felt he needed. Still the **fear** and **anxiety** persisted. Now John was suddenly **sad** and concerned, for usually **prayer** led him to **peace. Fear! Fear! Fear! Fear!** Why would his **fears** not subside?

Then John realized that he was not trusting **God** as he thought he did. He was asking **God** to **bless** the work of his hands but not truly leaving his **cares** and **concerns** in **God's** hands. He was not trusting **God** as deeply as he thought. John **prayed**, leaving all these matters in the hands of **God**, trusting Him to provide. Suddenly, as John had known so many times before, the **fear**, **anxiety**, and **sadness** lifted, and **peace** filled his entire being.

Have everyone let all the air out of their balloons.

Application: This illustration dramatically illustrates what stress, fear, and worry can do to people. They will also be reminded to entrust to God all matters of their life proactively, through prayer and faith. As the balloons get bigger and bigger, tension in the congregation will grow, and all will experience a measure of fear. This multisensory experience will help them to engage with your message on fear even more readily.

You can use this activity with some modification to speak on a variety of matters: the fear of God, handling stress, the meaning of success, the fear of death, priorities, faith, or trust in God.

....

TITLE: Potpourri

THEME: Becoming new in Christ

SCRIPTURE: 2 Corinthians 5:17

Related Passages: Ezekiel 36:26-27; Philippians 3:13; Romans 15:13; and Ephesians 1:18-19

Overview: This object lesson illustrates how God can take what is worthless in our lives and make it priceless.

Opener: Hold up two bags, one filled with dead leaves and wood shavings and the other with potpourri. Ask:

- What makes one bag worthless and the other worth $6.95?

Say: **Creative people are fascinating. People who can visualize a possibility where no one else sees anything are amazing. Architects, for example, have the ability to look at an empty lot, envision a beautiful structure, and actually *see* how it would look: its design—its lines—its windows—and even where you park.**

Because of this, I have always marveled at the invention of potpourri. This product proliferates in homes. Basically, it's a collection of leaves, twigs, and shavings scented and colored and placed in bowls around the home. How did someone think of this? Someone was undoubtedly raking leaves on their front lawn one fall day and thought, "Hey, I know what let's do. Instead of burning all these leaves and sticks and dead stuff, let's sprinkle perfume on it, spray it with colors, put it in a little cellophane bag with a ribbon and charge six bucks for it!"

This is what God does in us. He takes us as we are and sees the possibilities. We are lifeless leaves and sticks and shavings and dead stuff—destined only to be destroyed. But when God views us—being created in his image—he sees the possibilities still latent within us. And those possibilities are what moves him to save us.

Application: Consider asking the following questions before moving into your sermon:

- **When God wants to change a person, do you think he just sprays perfume and bright colors on that life and stops there? Why or why not?**
- **Do you ever think about changing anything in your life?**

Continue your sermon, stressing the importance of divine change in people's lives. Discuss how God can do this when we have a willing heart.

Section 3:
CREATIVE STORIES

TiTLe: Stained Glass Saints

THeMe: Sainthood

SCRipTURe: Colossians 1:12

Related Passages: Isaiah 58:8; Matthew 5:16; and Ephesians 3:17-18

Story: A young boy and his mother were visiting a cathedral in the south of France. Although much was unfamiliar to the boy, he recognized the beautiful stained glass as being similar to the windows of his own church.

As the boy paused to admire each window, his mother told him a brief story about the saint depicted in the art glass. "There," said his mother, "is Saint Francis, who loved all creatures, great and small. And over here is Saint Thomas Aquinas, who loved to learn about God." As they made their way down the aisle, stopping at each lovingly crafted frame, she introduced her young son to numerous heroes of the Christian faith.

When they arrived back at their hotel room, the boy's grandmother was eager to hear about his afternoon outing. "What did you do?" she asked.

"Oh, Grandmother!" he exclaimed. "I saw the beautiful windows of the cathedral. And each one was a different saint!"

"And what exactly is a saint?" she asked.

"You know, Grandma! They're those people the light shines through!"

Application: Consider asking the following questions before continuing your sermon:

- **How does the boy's definition of a saint fit with your traditional understanding of sainthood?**
- **According to the boy's definition, who has been a saint in your life this week?**
- **Are you comfortable with being addressed as a saint? Why or why not?**

TiTLe: A Smile and a Kind Word

THeMe: Poverty

SCRipTURe: James 5:1-9

Related Passages: Proverbs 14:31; Galatians 2:10; and 1 Timothy 5:3

Story: An actress who was playing a homeless bag lady spent several weeks on location in the downtown region of a major city far from Hollywood. One evening, as an exercise in understanding her character, she remained in costume long after the day's shoot had been completed.

It did not take long for her to notice the five o'clock passersby who looked in her direction and turned their heads. Children crossed to the other side of the street when their mothers bent to whisper in their ears. A bicyclist spat at her as he raced by—she heard his howling laughter half a block away. As the street lights came on, she felt her spirit sink lower and lower, even though she knew she was only a five-minute walk from a hot shower and scented luxury hotel room sheets. The darkness of the street began to claim her soul, even through the protective shield of a good education and a promising career. She wanted to shed her street costume, to run down the sidewalk screaming, "This is not what it looks like!"

As she fought off the near-panic state, chin tucked protectively to her chest, she nearly collided with a young man racing down the steps of a local church. "Good evening, ma'am," he said. "How are you tonight?"

He was at the curb before she even had a chance to answer but not before she took note of the clerical collar he was wearing.

The image was clear in her mind long after the movie passed through the theaters and into home video. Months later she recounted, "It was as though the simple tone of his voice lifted my head and made me stand tall. I realized that he thought I was a street person, yet he called me 'ma'am' as though he believed I was a teacher or a lawyer or an actress. I will never forget that his words gave me courage. I can never again pass a street person without acknowledging his or her presence. I may not be able to give anything but dignity, but I will pass along that gift forever. That man was God clothed in clerical garb for me that night, and I know I can be the same for another."

Application: Read James 5:1-9. Consider asking the following questions before continuing your sermon:

- **What is your greatest struggle with the poor?**
- **What acts of respect can you offer the poor?**
- **Why do you think God is so explicit about favoritism in the church?**

TiTLe: 'Tis So Sweet
THeMe: Trusting God
SCRiPTURe: Philippians 4:7
Related Passages: Job 12:13; Psalm 119:30; and Proverbs 3:5

Story: She was twenty-one, bright, and full of enthusiasm for her task. She had known since childhood that she was born to evangelize, and so she landed on the shores of the United States, poised for service. Four years later, she married. Soon she had a daughter—her lovely Lily—and her time was invested in the pleasures of life in the state of New York.

Picnicking along the shores of Long Island Sound one day, the family heard the gurgling shrieks of a drowning boy. Without thought for his own life, her husband raced into the water and became entrapped by the struggling youth and his own turn-of-the-century heavy clothing. Before his family's eyes, he disappeared under the waters of the sound.

Why? crowded every other thought from her mind. *Why him? Why now? Why here? Why me?* Gradually the questions were replaced by a peace she had never known. She processed her grief with a pencil in hand and penned these words:

'Tis so sweet to trust in Jesus, just to take Him at His word;

Just to rest upon His promise; just to know, "Thus saith the Lord."

The song became her legacy to the people of Zimbabwe, whom she went on to serve with confidence in the sufficiency of God. It continues to offer a testimony of survival for those who suddenly lose a child or are diagnosed with a fatal disease or face each day with the uncertainty of a prodigal loved one or who find themselves suddenly alone. Louisa M. R. Stead's words remind us that along the borders of our understanding, God offers something far sweeter: his peace.

Application: Consider asking these questions before continuing your sermon:

• **What keeps you from accepting the limits of your understanding?**

• **How can we deal with our "need to know"?**

• **How do you identify and accept God's peace even when you don't understand?**

TiTLe: Against All Odds

THeMe: Fallen world

SCRiPTURe: Genesis 3:14-19

Related Passages: John 8:42-47; Galatians 5:16-18; and 1 Thessalonians 2:13-17

Story: By the age of eleven, Mikey had been through more turmoil than most of us will ever face in a lifetime. His father had spent eight out of the eleven years of his life in jail for selling drugs, and when he was out of jail, was nowhere to be seen. His mother abused drugs and alcohol on a regular basis and spent many days and evenings in jail for various offenses. His fifteen-year-old brother was in a gang as well as his sister and her fiancé.

In a three-month period, Mikey was literally stabbed in the back over a sports jacket, assaulted several times at school, witnessed a drive-by shooting where a young man was killed, and saw his sister's fiancé get shot in the neck, doomed to spend the rest of his life as a quadriplegic. His lifetime of inconsistent parents and this summer of violence scarred Mikey in ways that his teachers at school, his mother, and others who cared about him really could not understand.

At eleven years old, Mikey would go to school about half of the time. When he did go, he would never talk to any teachers or any of the students in his classroom. One afternoon, his teacher set firm boundaries after a request, and Mikey responded in the way he had been taught when confronted with choices that he did not agree with. He threw his desk to the ground and picked up his chair and hurled it at his teacher.

After his school expulsion, Mikey was taken to several therapeutic classrooms with a very low teacher-student ratio. Eventually, Mikey assaulted somebody in every self-contained classroom that he was involved in. After several unsuccessful placements, Mikey was taken out of his home and placed in residential treatment, where he lived with other young boys who struggled with emotional expression. After approximately three days at the residential facility, Mikey ran away and has not been seen by his caseworker or the police since.

Application: Before you continue your sermon, ask your congregation to consider these questions:

- **What bothers you about Mikey's story?**
- **How has this fallen world negatively affected your life?**
- **How has your sinful nature negatively affected others?**
- **How can we communicate the love of God in the midst of the injustice all around us?**
- **How would you explain the love of God to Mikey? to his parents? to the person sitting next to you?**

....

TITLE: The Secret
THEME: New Year's resolutions
SCRIPTURE: Mark 4:26-28
Related Passages: 1 Corinthians 9:24; Philippians 1:6; and Hebrews 12:1

Story: Left motherless with an alcoholic father in the last decade of the nineteenth century, he grew to only five feet two inches, yet he earned the nickname "The Biggest Little Man in the Company." He was elected Sunday school superintendent more years in a row than anyone else before or since. He went into business with his best friend, who ran up thousands of dollars of debt during the Great Depression, then disappeared. He didn't sue. He worked off the debts, then sold the restaurant and barely broke even. When his friend returned to town, people asked him how he would treat the man. He said, "I'll treat him like he never went away." He buried two of his children. It broke his heart and cracked his spirit, but it didn't shake his faith.

People asked him about his recipe for successful Christian life. He always responded with characteristic humility and very little detail. The details he did give faded with age, and I remember him only from age eighty on. So it was years before I discovered the secret.

The box in the attic was dusty, the cardboard faded. I wiped the lid with a dust rag before I ever touched it. I lifted the lid and found a second box containing many brittle pages. The first was dated December 31, 1958, several years before my birth. I recognized his familiar penmanship, classically trained in the days before teachers distinguished between printing and cursive. It said: "Resolved, to be a better person on December 31, 1959, than I am today through prayer, Bible study, and service to my fellow man." I lifted the sheet and began to read the next one. It was dated December 31, 1957. It said "Resolved, to be a better person on December 31, 1958, than I am today though prayer, Bible study, and service to my fellow man."

I thought I might have misread the first page, so I compared the two. No mistake. I turned to the third page. It was dated December 31, 1956. It carried the identical message. I quickly thumbed through the rest of the stack. The bottom one was dated December 31, 1899. Fifty-nine years of the same resolution. Fifty-nine years of single-minded resolve. Fifty-nine years of determination that carried him through marriage, the loss of his children, a career among men twice his size, failed business ventures, retirement. Fifty-nine years of devotion to becoming God's man, line by line, page by page, step by step.

I learned a secret that day, as my tears made a path through time. The world moves at a faster pace now, but some things should never change.

Application: Consider asking the following questions before continuing your sermon:

- **What resolutions do you carry?**
- **How are those resolutions impacting your life?**
- **What secret legacy do you hope to leave for your grandchildren and great-grandchildren?**

....

TITLE: Love as God Loves
THEME: Love
SCRIPTURE: 1 John 4:7
Related Passages: John 13:34-35 and 15:13 and 1 John 3:16

Story: The sun had risen gloriously on the day of the wedding. Now it filled the room with a warm glow as Sheila put on her wedding dress. It was finally here—the day she and Brian had dreamed of and planned for so long.

Sheila hadn't expected to feel this way. It wasn't that she didn't want to get married. She was so excited she barely could contain herself. But she had so many other feelings pulling at her heart. And one in particular had struck her last night and nearly overwhelmed her today. When she thought about the future, she just felt so unsure.

Sheila looked around at the other women who were dressing and helping her get dressed. She listened to their chatter for a moment, as if trying to find an answer to her questions. They all seemed so happy and so at ease with this occasion.

Am I supposed to feel this way? she thought. *Is this normal? I'm so unsure about the future. What if I'm not a good wife? What if Brian isn't who I think he is? What if our love isn't strong enough to last? What if this marriage fails?*

"I'm so happy for you! You must be so excited!" Debbie's voice broke into Sheila's thoughts, and Sheila flashed a nervous smile. She looked in the mirror to adjust her veil, and she noticed her hands were shaking.

What if I'm not strong enough to make it through the trials in our future? she asked herself. *Can I live up to the promises I'm about to make?*

"Sheila, are you ready?"

Sheila turned and saw Grandma standing in the doorway. She looked around the room and saw that everyone else had left.

"They're going to start taking pictures now, dear. Are you ready?"

Sheila took a deep breath and started toward the door.

"It isn't you," Grandma said suddenly.

Sheila stopped and looked at Grandma in surprise.

"Everyone has doubts. You know yourself pretty well, and by now you know you aren't perfect. And I know you aren't naive enough to believe Brian is perfect either."

Sheila just stared at Grandma in astonishment. *How did she know?* she thought.

"Let me tell you something I've learned over the years: Love him the way God loves you," Grandma said. "You'll face some hard times, and you won't always feel as though you love him. But if you remember God's love for you and depend on God to help you love your husband, you'll have a wonderful marriage. Love Brian no matter how you feel, communicate, and forgive. Remember God's grace."

Grandma paused and then smiled tenderly. "Brian is a good man—and a lucky one."

"Thanks, Grandma," Sheila said. She gave Grandma a quick hug, being careful not to crush Grandma's corsage. Then she took another deep breath. "I'm ready for the pictures," she said with confidence. She took Grandma's arm and began walking down the hall.

After a few steps, Sheila stopped and looked at Grandma. "How did you know how I was feeling? Was it that obvious?"

"No," Grandma said. "I remember my wedding day."

Application: As you move into your sermon, consider asking these questions:

- **How would our marriages be different if we always loved each other the way God loves us?**
- **How would our families be different if we always loved each other the way God loves us?**
- **How would our church be different if we always loved each other the way God loves us?**

....

TITLE: Why?
THEME: Suffering
SCRIPTURE: Romans 8:28-39
Related Passages: Genesis 3:8-24; 2 Samuel 12:13-19; Job 38; and James 1:2-4

Story: It was like a bad dream. Mike had been laughing and playing with his family, enjoying a beautiful winter day. Now here he was, lying in a hospital bed, paralyzed from the waist down.

The doctors and nurses hurried in and out, filling the room with medical chatter. His wife, Sandie, stood nearby and spoke in low tones with the medical staff. Her face looked tired and worried—more than he had ever seen. His three daughters were nowhere to be seen. It was all so confusing.

Mike closed his eyes. He tried to take a deep breath, but he was stopped short by pain. *I can't believe this is happening*, he thought.

He tried to remember the events of the day: Skiing with his family. The sun shining brightly off the snow on the mountain. He and Sandie teaching their youngest daughter how to ski. Everyone excited as they began their first run.

About halfway down the mountain, it had happened. He had heard Sandie yell out his name, and he had looked up just in time to see the tree before he hit it. Then a blast of awful, intense pain.

Mike opened his eyes. He looked at his motionless body. Yes, it was real. It had happened. What could he have done differently? Could he have prevented this whole thing? If he hadn't been helping his daughter…No! It wasn't her fault. He couldn't even begin to think that way.

Whose fault was it? It was an accident. *Oh, God!* he cried silently. *Why? How could you let this happen? Aren't you supposed to take care of me and my family? Why me? Why did this happen?*

Mike felt a tear on his cheek and realized he was crying. He thought of Sandie and turned his head toward the window. He couldn't let her see him crying.

Everything is going to be different now, he thought. He couldn't go back to his job in construction. No more skiing with his daughters…*Stop!* he thought. *I can't think about that now!*

Mike tried to clear his head. He started to take another deep breath, and again he was startled by the intensity of his pain. "God, why?" he whispered. "Why?"

Application: As you move into your sermon, ask your congregation to recall a time when they suffered. Allow them several seconds of silence to remember how they felt at that time and to consider how that experience affected their relationship with God.

Then continue your sermon, focusing on why bad things happen in our lives. You may want to highlight some biblical examples, such as Job or David, and outline some reasons God might allow suffering in our lives.

....

TITLE: Lessons on God's Love From Disneyland
THEME: God's love
SCRIPTURE: 1 John 3:1
Related Passages: Psalm 86:5; Jeremiah 31:3; Romans 5:8; and 1 Timothy 1:16

Story: He's four years old, and he does *not* want to go and watch *Honey, I*

Shrunk the Audience movie in 3-D. He wants to ride the boats in Storybook Land, and since he's only four, he believes if he doesn't ride the boats *now,* he will never be able to ride them.

Because the adults with him are already in line for the 3-D movie and they know they can ride the boats in Storybook Land later (when the Storybook Land ride will actually be open), the adults insist.

The four-year-old will teach them! He pulls out his biggest guns of displeasure—pouting, frowning, and being contrarily unpleasant. The adults recognize this arsenal. They have used those weapons themselves.

The four-year-old refuses to watch those entertaining the waiting audience. He refuses to look at the humorous video that explains what's about to take place—though he had a close call. He found himself almost enjoying a short cartoon. Fortunately, he caught himself just in time and fired another salvo of personal annoyance. That was close!

Upon entering the theater, everyone is issued the special 3-D glasses needed to get the full effect. The four-year-old takes his glasses—they are kind of spiffy looking with bright yellow frames—but he refuses to put them on.

The movie begins. The 3-D effects are stunning and realistic. Characters seem to leap from the screen into your lap. The audience ducks and screams at the apparent "near misses" of flying objects, dogs, and debris zooming out from the screen only inches from their faces. The people roar with laughter at the slapstick comedic moments.

All except the four-year-old. Despite repeated encouragement to do so, he refuses to place the glasses on his face. What he sees is a large screen showing fuzzy figures outlined in green, red, and blue.

They do not "zoom." There is no illusion they are going to leap into his lap. He sees nothing but a TV-type picture that looks as if the picture tube is failing. He never allows himself to put on his glasses, and so he never knows the fun he missed.

Later in the day, on the Storybook Land boat ride, he may have thought he got to ride the boats because of his stubbornness at the theater. If he had been given to such thinking, he probably would have decided he had won.

But now none of that mattered. He was riding in the boats! He was going to eat in Goofy's Kitchen!…go on Mr. Toads' Wild Ride!…and spend hours playing in the fountain in Tomorrowland! Whether he realized it or not, he was enjoying it all—not because he tried to punish the adults and they finally folded—but because they love him more than rest or money—in spite of his occasional bad behavior.

Application: Consider sharing the following comments before moving into your sermon:

The love of the adults for this four-year-old is a pale reflection of God's love for us. However, we do find ourselves a little uncomfortable as we observe this child's actions and attitudes in the face of delay. Can this be us when we don't receive the answers or the timing we desire from God?

TITLE: Thoughts in the Dentist's Chair
THEME: The tongue
SCRIPTURE: James 3:8-9
Related Passages: Proverbs 12:14; 13:3; 15:1, 2, 4; 16:24, 28; 17:20; and 18:7

Story: "OK, now relax your tongue. I'm going to move it to the side," the dental hygienist instructed. Relax my tongue? Is that possible? I try to remember what a relaxed tongue feels like…there, I think I've got it.

"Please sir, you have to relax your tongue. I can't see the tooth with your tongue in the way." Oops! I guess that wasn't it. This is not as easy as it sounds. Half of my mouth is numb, including my tongue. I can't really tell if it's tense, relaxed, or has completely left town.

I sense she is pushing on something. Could be my tongue…can't really tell. I think I'm moving it in the direction she's pushing. It seems to satisfy her.

"Thank you," she says.

I respond with a gargling, "You're welcome."

What is there about the tongue that makes it so difficult to control? Obviously, it can be trained. We learn to speak words, make noises, sing, yell, and eat.

But when someone, even ourselves, places a finger in our mouth and tries to move it aside, it takes a serious concentrated effort to make it happen, if at all. The harder we push, the more it resists. We have to make a definite decision and issue a direct order to get it to respond. And even then, we don't push it so much as we stay against it as it moves. The tongue obviously is influenced by things other than surface ideas.

Application: Consider asking the following questions before continuing your sermon:

- **Have you ever said anything negative about someone and wished you hadn't?**
- **What do you think this means:"When words are many, sin is not absent"?**
- **What is the best guarantee of a conversation and communication style that will always give glory to God?**

....

TITLE: Graffiti
THEME: Living for Jesus
SCRIPTURE: Ephesians 5:1
Related Passages: Matthew 19:13-14; Mark 6:31-34; and John 15:9-13

Story: The pastor pulled into his parking space of the downtown church. It was very early with the sun offering a feeble introduction to the coming dawn. Before getting out of the car, he turned off the engine and was mentally going over the tasks of the day ahead.

Suddenly he noticed something on the white wall of the church in front of him. Bringing his attention back to the immediate, he could see that someone had been busy in the night with a can of black spray paint. Involuntarily, he began to feel a flush of frustration, anger, and helplessness. It was then he saw that the graffiti "artists" had been trying to leave a message. He spelled it out: "S-A-N-T-A-N-L-I-V-E-S!!!" Santan? Santan? Was this the work of some weird followers of Santa Claus? The Santans?

Further down the wall he spelled out:"S-A-T-I-N-L-I-V-E-S!" Satin? *Maybe some activist interior decorator is laying down the law of a fabric preference*, he thought with a growing smile.

Of course, there was no doubt what the spray painters had meant to say. They had meant to declare their defiance by painting on the wall of the church that "Satan Lives" but were defeated because they couldn't spell.

Application: Consider asking the following questions before continuing your sermon:

- **The Apostle Paul wrote in Galatians 6:17, "I bear on my body the marks of Jesus." Where do we leave our marks for Christ?**
- **Is our message clear or confusing?**
- **When people read what I say with my life, do they learn how to spell "Jesus"? Why or why not?**

....

TITLE: Tough Talk
THEME: Careless words
SCRIPTURE: Proverbs 25:11
Related Passages: Psalm 109:1-5 and Proverbs 11:13; 12:18; 15:1, and 18:23

Story: The story is told of a man who boards an airplane, locates his assigned seat, and is buckling his seat belt when he notices the seat next to him is occupied by a parrot.

After takeoff the flight attendant comes by and asks if there is anything they would like to drink. The man politely asks for a cup of coffee, but the parrot rudely says, "You can get me a diet cola and be quick about it!"

The flight attendant immediately hurries up the aisle and returns with the diet cola, but no coffee. She asks if there will be anything else, and the man politely repeats his request for a cup of coffee, but the parrot asks harshly, "Where are the peanuts? Are you stupid or something? Get me some peanuts!"

The flight attendant quickly returns with the bag of peanuts. Still no coffee. It's obvious to the man that his courtesy is getting him nowhere. In desperation he decides he'll adopt the demanding, aggressive attitude of the parrot. "Listen, jet-fuel-for-brains, I'm telling you for the last time, get me a cup of coffee and be quick about it!"

The flight attendant returns up the aisle and walks past the galley into the pilot's compartment. Soon a huge copilot comes out, walks down the aisle, grabs both the man and the parrot, takes them to the rear door, kicks it open, and throws them out of the plane.

As they are falling, the parrot, flapping his wings, turns to the man and says; "That was pretty tough talk for someone who can't fly."

Application: Consider asking the following questions before moving into your sermon:

- **Did you ever think about words being living and powerful, taking on a life of their own? Why or why not?**
- **Have you ever said something you wish you could take back?**
- **Have you ever been devastated by the remarks someone made about you or to you?**

STORY: For Sale

THEME: Commitment

SCRIPTURE: Psalm 102:25-28

Related Passages: Psalm 112:6-8; John 15:4-7; and Hebrews 10:22-23, 35-36

Story: "For Sale: Brand-new Porsche 911SC Targa, 2,300 miles. $50." Since the actual value of the vehicle was around $60,000, the interested party assumed the $50 was a newspaper typo. He called the number and went to take a look.

The lady met him at the door and pressed the garage door button to reveal a car exactly as advertised; coal-black, glistening under the garage lights with that "new car" smell emanating from the interior. He looked at the odometer. It read 2,304 miles. It was gorgeous.

He asked, "How much?"

She responded, "Like the paper said, fifty dollars."

He laughed appreciatively at her little joke. "Ha, ha. No, really, how much are you asking?"

She wasn't laughing. She said evenly, "Fifty dollars and it's yours."

Convinced, but still uncertain, he asked, "But why…?"

She took a deep breath and said, "Look, my husband ran off with his secretary. He sent me a telegram telling me our marriage was over and instructing me to sell the Porsche and send him the money. The price is fifty dollars."

Application: Say: **There's a certain "deliciousness" about this story. We find it difficult to resist licking our lips in satisfaction when overbearing arrogance is rewarded with a delightfully surgical comeuppance.**

But we also notice that there is pain here. What one person thought was commitment turned out to be only a transaction of temporary value in effect until the arrival of a higher bidder.

Consider asking these questions before you move into your sermon:

- **Have you ever had promises made to you by someone you loved and trusted, only to be betrayed?**
- **Have you ever prayed and made promises to God in a crisis that you later ignored when the immediate pressure was off?**

TITLE: Jesus Knows Your Name
THEME: God's love
SCRIPTURE: Isaiah 43:1-5a
Related Passages: 1 Kings 19:9-18; John 20:11-16; and Acts 9:1-4

Story: With love, he watched his daughter as she was getting ready to leave the house. He knew that along with everything else, a relationship had come to an end, and she was feeling depressed, discouraged, unloved, unappreciated, and fed up.

She was standing inside the front door, collecting her purse and keys as she juggled her schoolbooks and coffee in the balancing act we use to face the day. Life itself was making her feel insignificant and, frankly, it didn't care.

He sensed she needed to know she was important and special. Impulsively he called out to her, "Hold it!"

She stopped, startled. "What?"

He said, "Put down the coffee, the purse, the keys, and your books."

Looking a little exasperated, she did so.

He took her in his arms, held her in a big hug, and said, "I just want you to know that I love you and I think you are wonderful. I'm very proud of you and, believe it or not, Kara, life does get better."

She gratefully returned her father's hug with a chuckle and said, "Thanks

Dad, I love you too, but I'm the other one. My name is Erika."

Application: Consider asking the following questions before moving into your sermon:

- **How do you feel when you are in a large crowd of strangers?**
- **Have you ever wondered if God knows or cares who you are, where you are, or what's happening in your life?**
- **Do you think God ever gets you mixed up with someone else?**

Continue by exploring the promises of God's faithfulness and personal involvement in our lives.

TITLE: God's Positioning System
THEME: Christian living
SCRIPTURE: John 12:50
Related Passages: Romans 2:4; 6:19, 22-23; 12:2; Ephesians 4:20-24; 1 Timothy 6:11-12; and 1 John 1:5-7

Story: "Where are we?" is a common question when we're traveling through unfamiliar territory. Navigation is important to people who want to know where they are in relation to where they have been and where they're going.

Early navigational aids were as basic as the early forms of travel. Walking, for instance, gave one considerable time to think about navigation and to decide where to go—"I'll walk to the top of the next hill and see what's ahead." The speed of travel today rarely allows us the time for such reflection.

There is a system of navigational satellites that orbits the earth at about 10,900 miles. It is called the Global Positioning System, and anyone who possesses a special GPS receiver can receive information for navigational purposes.

When activated, your hand-held receiver will calculate the satellites' positions in orbit relative to your position on the ground and immediately tell you, within a few feet, exactly where you are on the face of the earth.

What technology has done for the physical world, God has done for the spiritual journey. GPS could just as easily stand for *God's* Positioning System. The presence of the Holy Spirit in our lives acts as a constant spiritual navigational system. What should I do? How should I be? God's Positioning System never fails to give us the correct direction and position.

In a world lost in dead reckoning, we can always know exactly where we are. All that's required is that you activate the system. Even God's Positioning System won't work until you turn it on.

Application: Consider asking these questions before moving into your sermon:
- **Are you reluctant to ask directions when you're not sure where you're going? Why or why not?**
- **Are you reluctant to ask directions from God when you're not sure where you're going in life? Why or why not?**

TITLE: Cougar!
THEME: Running from God
SCRIPTURE: 1 John 4:9-10
Related Passages: Isaiah 54:10; Lamentations 3:22; and John 3:16

Story: "Cougar! Cougar! Help! Cougar!" Marvin screamed at the top of his lungs as he ran toward the lights at the edge of town.

It was dark when Marvin, ten years old, had started the walk from his home in the foothills into the small town. There was no moon, and he could tell he was still on the road only by the familiar crunch of the gravel beneath his feet.

Suddenly, in the distance he heard the unmistakable screeching cry of a cougar. He stopped dead still. He could feel the hair on the back of his neck begin to stiffen.

As he walked on, the first cougar's cry was answered by another somewhat nearer. Marvin began to walk a little faster. It was then he heard other footsteps in the gravel behind him. He turned around quickly but could see nothing in the dark. He began to jog.

The footsteps were still behind and had matched his pace. A porch light from an empty house weakly penetrated the darkness. He stopped again. He looked back and made out the dim silhouette of an animal standing in the road looking at him.

He turned toward town and saw the safe lights of houses up ahead. He began to run for his life! The footsteps behind were rapidly catching up. In his fear he could feel the hot breath of the mountain lion on his neck. He expected at any second to be taken down by its claws.

He was crying, running, praying, wishing he could fly! He began to cry out, "Cougar! Cougar! Help! Cougar!"

Men and women who had been sitting on their front porches in the summer darkness heard him, and suddenly he was surrounded by townspeople with guns and lights ready to shoot the animal.

As Marvin turned in terror to point down the dark road, his dog, Brownie, came up panting from the long run, jumped into his arms, and licked his face.

Application: Share these thoughts before continuing your sermon: **Francis Thompson wrote one of the greatest lyrical poems in the English language with the allegorical title *The Hound of Heaven*. In this poem, Thompson wrote of hearing footsteps pursue him in the dark, always assuming that it's a threat, something to fear, some disaster closing:**

> *Halts by me that footfall*
> *Is my gloom, after all,*
> *(the) shade of His hand,*
> *outstretched, caressingly?*
> *"Ah, fondest, blindest, weakest,*
> *I am He Whom thou seekest.*
> *You drove love from thee, when you fled*
> *from me."*

Only God's love pursues us unrelentingly from cradle to grave.

TITLE: Treed
THEME: Unnecessary fear
SCRIPTURE: 1 Timothy 1:7
Related Passages: Job 28:28; Psalm 89:48; Jeremiah 1:17; and Hebrews 13:5-6

Story: Vic and Joan Waters live in the foothills of the Sierra Nevada mountains in northern California. Television reception is poor, and for various reasons, neither cable nor satellite dish is available. A man named Paul had developed a good business installing television antennae in the tops of trees in order to increase the quality of reception.

Mr. and Mrs. Waters were leaving for a two-week vacation, and Paul had agreed to install a TV antenna in a tall pine tree about two hundred feet from their house during their absence.

Paul—busy with other installations—suddenly realized two weeks had slipped by and the Waters would be back from vacation the next day. He hurried out to their place, climbed the tree, and in a couple of hours the work was finished.

Scrambling down, he glanced across the small clearing in front of the house. A mountain lion was strolling out of the trees! The lion stopped to sniff Paul's truck, then headed directly for Paul's tree.

Paul froze as the big cat squinted up into the branches. When it became distracted by some of the trash piled nearby, Paul began easing back up the tree—climbing as high as he could. He tried to remember, *Did mountain lions climb trees?* He was sure they did.

Paul had a problem. Mountain lions in the foothills were a very real threat—people had been attacked and sometimes killed. If he tried to climb down and run for his truck, the cat could take him down easily before he got fifty feet from the tree, or he might come up the tree after him.

He thought of yelling for help, but he was too far from the road to be heard. Besides, he really didn't want to increase the lion's curiosity concerning what was in the top of the tree. So he waited, uncomfortable on a limb that seemed to become harder and smaller by the hour.

As the day passed, the mountain lion nosed around, occasionally looking up into the tree, and finally stretched out at its base. When the sun set and darkness came, Paul, using antenna] wire, wired himself to the tree so he wouldn't fall in his sleep. He spent the most miserable night of his life. The moon shone clearly. He could see the mountain lion on the ground below him—sleeping, rummaging, growling, purring, but never leaving!

The next morning about 10, a car came down the driveway. The cat immediately stirred, crouching in a pounce position behind some weeds as the car came to a stop. Mr. and Mrs. Waters got out, unaware of the danger just behind them.

Paul cried out, "Look out! There's a mountain lion right behind you!"

Mrs. Waters turned and looked up into the tree at Paul, "Oh, hello, Paul. The antenna looks beautiful."

Paul yelled again, "Look out! There's a mountain lion crouched down in those weeds there! Get back in the car! Get some help!"

Mrs. Waters looked over at the weeds. She saw the top of the lion's head pointing her way. "Oh", she said, "that's just old Willy. He's so old he doesn't have any teeth left. He's hanging around so I'll feed him. Go on, Willy, now scat!" She waved her arms in the air, and the lion jumped up, running off into the woods.

Application: Consider asking the following questions before moving into your sermon:

- **How often are we treed by toothless fears?**
- **Have you noticed how paralyzing fear can be?**
- **What happens when we give in to our fears?**

TITLE: Cookies
THEME: Knowing the future
SCRIPTURE: 2 Timothy 1:12
Related Passages: 2 Samuel 12:1-19; Matthew 6:33; and Acts 20:22-24

Story: On the whole Jake can categorically state that he likes cookies. He had never really had a *bad* cookie. He's had good cookies and great cookies and cookies that passed greatness and moved into the *sublime* of "cookieness," redefining by their texture, taste, and sheer visual appeal what God must have had in mind when he first thought "cookie."

Jake has even pondered that world peace would be less elusive if we would refocus. For instance, if the evening news would bring us less information about the White House and more news about the Toll House, what a better world this would be.

Jake and his wife were finishing dinner at their favorite Chinese restaurant. It was fortune cookie time. Fortune cookies bring two delights: taste to savor and a tale to tell. Jake's fortune said, "You will soon be lavishly rewarded for your hard work."

Now Jake knows there is nothing to this. He knows that these fortunes are churned out in some print shop with no regard to consulting anything that would give this statement credibility. But, in fact, he felt his heart leap a little at the prospect. The little note came from the far side of the possible—and who knows?—maybe it would come true.

Jake's fortune cookie optimism was based on experience. His wife once had broken open a cookie and the fortune said, "You are extremely shy about visiting nude beaches." He could vouch for the truth of that statement. "If the cookie can be right about that," he rationalized, "then isn't it possible that it *may* be right about my being 'lavishly rewarded' "?

We look everywhere for signs of what's going to happen to us. Astrology, tea leaves, and fortune cookies are just some of the more common mediums chosen. We have, however, a more reliable source concerning our future.

Application: Consider asking these questions before moving into your sermon:

- **Do you get caught up in the "what's" of life? What's going to happen? What am I going to do? What now? What's next?**
- **How might this verse quiet the "what's" in life—"Do not be afraid...for your Father has been pleased to give you the kingdom" (Luke 12:32)?**

TITLE: Testing...Testing...
THEME: Trials and tests
SCRIPTURE: James 1:2-3, 12
Related Passages: 2 Corinthians 4:6-12 and 11:22-33

Story: "Swan Lake is frozen, we can skate!" The word went out in the high school where Jack was a sophomore. He had moved to the area the summer before with his parents.

Swan Lake did not freeze every winter, so the fact that it was frozen now created a lot of excitement. Jack had never been ice-skating anywhere, much less on a genuine frozen lake, so he couldn't wait.

Jack didn't give the lake much thought until he found himself in the middle. It was then that he began to think about the ice and the water beneath.

With increasing anxiety he began to wonder how thick the ice was beneath his skates and how thick the ice should be in order to be thick enough. He didn't have a clue.

Suddenly realizing he was pretty much alone in the center of the lake, he looked up to see other people skating some distance away. He also noticed that someone had driven a car onto the ice near the shore.

With mounting fear he headed for the car, figuring that the ice must surely be thick enough to be safe where it was. Rational thought completely fled. Jack was gripped by overwhelming panic as he found himself stumbling, running, sort of skating, while trying to levitate himself against gravity so as to not put any undue pressure on the ice's fragile surface.

He heard the ice crack before he saw it. A sharp brittle sound with a deadly bass echo. The sound of doom! Almost immediately the crack snaked across the ice in front of him like the jagged finger of a bolt of lightning. He stopped as still as a terrified statue, his heart in his throat. He stood frozen in place, waiting for the shock of the icy water to engulf him, afraid to even shift his vision for fear he would go down faster.

Suddenly, he saw a movement and risked death by refocusing his eyes. Standing in front of him was Daniel, a friend from school.

He said, "You okay, Jack?"

Eyes wide with fright, Jack shouted, "Look out! The ice! It's breaking!"

Daniel answered, "What? Oh, the crack? That's just a pressure crack. As the lake keeps freezing, the ice expands. No big deal. You want to go get some hot chocolate?"

What Jack thought was the sound of ice failure was actually the sound of the ice becoming stronger.

Application: Consider asking these questions before moving into your sermon:

- **Have you experienced times when it seemed as though the thing you feared the most was happening to you and out of that you learned wonderful lessons of God's love and support?**
- **What did that experience teach you about the purpose of trials and tests in life?**

TITLE: Lessons From a Little Princess

THEME: Christian growth

SCRIPTURE: Hebrews 5:11-14

Related Passages: Philippians 3:7-10 and 2 Peter 3:18

Story: She is a beautiful princess. Her head is crowned with a tiara covered with sparkling jewels and diamonds. It rests in the curled locks of spun gold that is her hair. She's dressed in costly silk, the color of a blushing sunrise, and on her feet are slippers lovingly crafted of the finest leather.

Her clear blue eyes are filled with tears. Obviously all is not well in her kingdom.

Her mother has her by the arm and is propelling her out the front door of the supermarket. She is explaining to the princess, in undiplomatic terms, that she can *not* have any Skittles because she has just thrown a tantrum.

The nearby observer laughs quietly and unobtrusively, but the princess sees him and is infuriated. She stamps her lovingly crafted ballet slippers in frustration as the tiara bounces on her golden hair.

Meanwhile the observer is thinking to himself, *I'm sorry, princess. I know how you feel. I've felt that way myself when I didn't get what I wanted, and all I got were speeches, admonitions, and instructions.*

I no longer stamp my feet, not in public anyway; someone may see me and laugh. I stamp my feet on the inside and create a furrow in which to plant my selfishness, a garden for resentment and bitterness to grow, fertilized by my complaints.

The princess, with sparkling sequins in her hair and a parent's love surrounding her world, dries her tears, blows her nose, and follows her mother back into the store. She is protected, loved, and disciplined.

Not unlike myself and my heavenly Father, the observer muses, *who dries my tears and blows my nose after my internal tantrum because I have been denied some of life's "candy." He loves me, but I can sense his disappointment. After all, I'm not seven years old.*

Application: Consider sharing the following comments before moving into your sermon:

The Bible doesn't speak of "candy" as such, but it does talk about Jesus'

call to be childlike using "milk" and "solid food" as examples. It's the call to "grow up" as believers and residences of the living Christ, a call to move beyond our preoccupation with our personal preferences and seek earnestly, prayerfully what God would have us do—what he would have us risk, accomplish, and envision for his church.

....

TITLE: Tether Ball
THEME: Focus on Christ
SCRIPTURE: Psalm 141:8
Related Passages: Acts 9:1-9, 17-19; Romans 8:31-39; and Philippians 3:13-14

Story: Do you remember playing tether ball in school? The principles of the game were simple enough. A ball was attached by a rope to the top of a pole. The object was to hit the ball in such a way as to wrap the rope around the pole in your direction before your opponent did the opposite.

There was a lot of pain associated with the game for a boy named Billy. At the crucial "tether" moment, he would lash out with a powerful fist to strike the final blow that would send the ball spinning into orbit beyond the reach of his opponent only to have his fist connect, not with the ball, but with the steel buckle attached to the ball.

As he bent over in pain, his opponent, who always seemed to be some grade-school girl, would slam the ball into the stratosphere, completely wrapping the rope within the top six inches of the pole. Occasionally, he would make a great first serve, and while he was congratulating himself, the ball would come around and smack him in the back of the head.

There was no doubt Billy had a problem with the game. He didn't understand the basic principle—keep your eyes on the ball!

Application: Consider sharing the following comments before moving into your sermon:

Life can be a lot like tether ball: If you don't understand the basic principle—to keep your eyes on Jesus—you'll suffer pain and defeat.

TITLE: Sleeping With Scorpions
THEME: Consequence of sin
SCRIPTURE: Galatians 6:7-8
Related Passages: 1 Corinthians 10:12-13 and 1 John 1:9

Story: Few people seemed to know his real name or age. Everyone just called him "Slusher," which is the job description for someone loading ore into an ore car in an underground mine. He was the kind of person who looks ancient when you're a child, and when you see him forty years later, he looks the same. He lived in the desert in buildings and trailers that had been abandoned.

Southeastern California is a harsh landscape of desert valleys and towering mountain ranges of battered stone with little or no vegetation, a uniquely beautiful habitat for some of nature's most dangerous snakes and insects. It's a highly mineralized region and has been the focus of continuous mining and prospecting since it was first explored two hundred years ago.

One day Slusher came into the hospital complaining of a nasty scorpion bite on his arm. While the doctor treated him, Slusher explained how it came about.

Evidently he had been working a mining claim out near Death Valley and staying in an abandoned mining shack nearby. He had found an old sleeping bag there and was using it.

"I've seen thousands of scorpions and they never bothered me," Slusher said. "I woke up a couple of times while I was a-sleepin'. I knew the scorpion was in bed with me. The dog knew it too, but we didn't think it would bite."

Application: Consider asking these questions before moving into your sermon:
• **How is having a scorpion in your bed like having a hidden sin in your life?**
• **What sins are you in bed with?**
• **Just because you know your own sins very well, does that mean they are not without consequence?**

TITLE: Too Busy to Hear
THEME: Listening to God

SCRIPTURE: Psalm 46:10

Related Passages: Deuteronomy 5:27 and James 1:19

Story: In a small rural town during a time of high unemployment, a group of applicants gathered in the lobby of a company that had advertised having a position of employment. The group became so engaged in discussion and laughter that hardly a word could be heard over them. In fact, the sound was so loud that the applicants didn't hear the voice that came over the loudspeaker, except for one older gentleman. The man stood and walked through a door and into an office. A short time later, he happily appeared back in the lobby. When questioned by those waiting to be interviewed, he explained that one of them could have been hired had they listened to the voice over the loudspeaker.

"What voice?" they asked.

"The voice over the speaker," answered the man, "that said, 'I need an employee who is careful to listen for my instructions. The first one to hear this and come to my office will receive the job.'"

Application: Consider asking these questions before moving into your sermon:

- **In what ways does society today make hearing God's voice difficult?**
- **What are some different ways God speaks to us?**
- **How can we as Christians better prepare ourselves to hear and obey God's Word in the midst of the "noise" around us?**

TITLE: Does Forgiveness Have a Limit?

THEME: Forgiving others

SCRIPTURE: Luke 6:35-36

Related Scripture: Matthew 5:7; 6:12-15; and 18:21-33 and Luke 23:31

Story: Simon Wiesenthal was a Jewish prisoner in a concentration camp during World War II. He suffered much at the hands of the Nazis but not as much as some of his friends and family who lost their lives in very cruel ways. One particular day Simon was taken away from his work group to speak to a dying SS soldier. The dying soldier wanted to confess his atrocities and sins to

Simon. The soldier told Simon about specific instances when he had been ordered to kill Jewish families and complied. The soldier asked Simon to forgive him. The man appeared to be truly repentant of his sins and wanted to confess to Simon, who for him represented all Jews.

Simon was faced with a very difficult choice between compassion and justice. Simon decided to say nothing and left the soldier's bedside. The soldier died sometime during the night. Simon was often haunted by the memory of the soldier and wondered whether he had done the right thing.

Simon's choice wasn't as simple as it sounds. The issue at stake wasn't only whether Simon could forgive the soldier personally but whether he had the right to forgive him in the name of the victims who had died at the hands of the soldier.

Story adapted from Simon Wiesenthal, *The Sunflower: On the Possibilities and Limits of Forgiveness* (Schocken Books: New York, 1998.)

Application: Consider asking the following questions before continuing your sermon:

- **What would you have done had you been in Simon's place?**
- **Are there limits to forgiveness? Why or why not?**
- **What do you think Jesus would have done in Simon's place?**

TITLE: The Old Stone Archway
THEME: Eternal life
SCRIPTURE: Ecclesiastes 3:11
Related Passages: John 3:14-16 and 10:27-28 and Romans 6:23

Story: When Eigel was a small boy, every Saturday morning he would walk with his grandfather to the bakery. The old brick road they traveled was narrow and shaded by many trees. There was scarcely anyone else out at that time of morning. After what always seemed to Eigel to be a long walk, they would pass beneath an old stone archway that served as a bridge over the road. It was then that he would know they were near their journey's end.

One morning, just as they were walking under the archway, Eigel noticed a small dead rabbit beside the road. He stopped for a moment to look at it. His grandfather, noticing the young boy standing compassionately over the rabbit, walked to his side and put his arm around him.

"It's so small, Grandpa. Why did it live such a short life?" asked the young boy.

Eigel's grandfather paused for a moment and then answered, "In many ways, Eigel, our lives, too, will be short like this young rabbit's. But we must not labor too long with these earthly matters; instead we must think of spending eternity with God."

"But how long shall I live, Grandpa, and how long is eternity?"

"Look up at that old archway, my young Eigel. Each time we journey along this road, we walk beneath its shadow. Think about how quickly we pass beneath it. Your life, Eigel, is much like walking beneath the archway. God's eternity is like the rest of the journey. Our lives are short, and we must make the best of them. But God's eternity is much greater. And that, Eigel, is where our hearts and minds must be focused."

Application: Consider asking the following questions before moving into your sermon:

- **In what ways does life seem too short, almost like passing beneath an archway?**
- **In what ways does life seem too long?**
- **Why is it important to focus on the things of eternity rather than things of this world?**

TITLE: Just One Fish Stick
THEME: God's provision
SCRIPTURE: Philippians 4:19
Related Passages: Exodus 16:11-18; Proverbs 3:5-6; and 1 Peter 5:7

Story: Jill and Michael were doing their best to serve the Lord. Michael was in college, studying for the ministry, and Jill was working to pay the bills. Married only a few months, they struggled to make ends meet.

One week was particularly bleak. On Tuesday, the only food left in their mobile home was a single frozen fish stick and a few cans of vegetables. No money was due to come in before Friday, and in the early '70s, students didn't have credit cards. Jill and Michael had a few dollars, but they had to choose between buying gas for the car so that Michael could get to school and buying much-needed groceries. They bought the gas, trusting God would take care of them somehow.

Feeling a bit discouraged, Jill sat down to look through some brides' magazines she'd bought before the wedding. She was preparing to pass them on to her sister who was getting married within the year. As she flipped through the magazines, a slip of paper fluttered to the floor. Picking it up, Jill began to cry. It was a check for twenty-five dollars that they'd received months earlier as a wedding gift. It wasn't a lot, but it was all Jill and Michael needed to make it to Friday's paycheck. And they praised God together for his provision as they ate hamburgers that evening.

Application: Consider asking the following questions before continuing your sermon:

- **How often do you really trust God to provide for your needs?**
- **Why is it often easier to trust God when we have little?**

TITLE: **Aunt Blanche**
THEME: God's nature
SCRIPTURE: Exodus 34:6-7
Related Passages: Psalm 23; Isaiah 9:6; and 1 John 4:7-10

Story: Aunt Blanche was a dear old soul. But to five-year-old Paul, she was a very, very old woman. And when she arrived for a visit, it usually meant Mom and Dad were going away for a while and were leaving Paul with her.

Aunt Blanche was generally kind and gentle, laughing with Paul as she read a story or played a game. But when it came to nap time or bedtime, everything became serious business. Paul would be put in his bed, and Aunt Blanche would lie across the end of the bed until Paul was asleep, to make sure no funny business went on.

One day, Paul lay awake in his bed at nap time but pretended to sleep. *If she goes to sleep, I can sneak out,* he thought. And he lay quietly, waiting what seemed an eternity. When he decided that she was finally asleep, Paul slipped quietly from under the covers and onto the floor. But just as he tiptoed toward the door, Aunt Blanche—without stirring or opening her eyes—said sternly, "Get back in bed, young man."

Paul marveled at how she knew that he was trying to escape and determined right then and there that God must be a lot like Aunt Blanche.

Application: Consider asking the following questions before continuing your sermon:

- **How was Paul's Aunt Blanche similar to God? How was she different?**
- **Who is the "Aunt Blanche" in your past?**
- **What errant views of God did you carry from your childhood?**

TITLE: Extreme Living
THEME: Positive attitude
SCRIPTURE: Philippians 4:4
Related Passages: Nehemiah 8:10 and Philippians 3:1

Story: Jeff was the kind of guy you love to hate. He was always in a good mood and always had something positive to say. When someone would ask him how he was doing, he would reply, "If I were any better, I would be twins!" He was a unique manager because he had several waiters who had followed him around from restaurant to restaurant. The reason the waiters followed Jeff was because of his attitude. He was a natural motivator. If an employee was having a bad day, Jeff was there telling the employee how to look on the positive side of the situation.

Seeing this style really made me curious, so one day I said to Jeff, "I don't get it! You can't be positive all of the time. How do you do it?"

Jeff replied, "Each morning I wake up and say to myself, 'Jeff, you have two choices today. You can choose to be in a good mood, or you can choose to be in a bad mood.' I choose to be in a good mood. Each time something bad happens, I can choose to be a victim, or I can choose to learn from it. I choose to learn from it. Every time someone comes to me complaining, I can choose to accept their complaining, or I can point out the positive side of life. I choose the positive side of life."

"Yeah, right. It's not that easy," I protested.

"Yes, it is," Jeff said. "Life is all about choices. When you cut away all the junk, every situation is a choice. You choose how you react to situations. You choose how people will affect your mood. You choose to be in a good mood or bad mood. The bottom line: It's your choice how you live life."

I reflected on what Jeff had said. Soon thereafter, I left the restaurant industry to start my own business. We lost touch, but I often thought about him when I made a choice about life instead of reacting to it.

Several years later, I heard that Jeff did something you are never supposed to do in a restaurant business. He left the back door open one morning and was held up at gunpoint by three armed robbers. While trying to open the safe, his hand, shaking from nervousness, slipped off the combination. The robbers panicked and shot him. Luckily, Jeff was found relatively quickly and rushed to the local trauma center. After eighteen hours of surgery and weeks of intensive care, Jeff was released from the hospital with fragments of the bullets still in his body.

I saw Jeff about six months after the accident. When I asked him how he was, he said, "If I were any better, I'd be twins. Wanna see my scars?"

I declined to see his wounds, but I did ask him what had gone through his mind as the robbery took place.

"The first thing that went through my mind was that I should have locked the back door," Jeff replied. "Then, as I lay on the floor, I remembered that I had two choices: I could choose to live, or I could choose to die. I chose to live."

"Weren't you scared? Did you lose consciousness?" I asked.

Jeff continued, "The paramedics were great. They kept telling me I was going to be fine. But when they wheeled me into the emergency room and I saw the expressions on the faces of the doctors and nurses, I got really scared. In their eyes, I read, 'He's a dead man.' I knew I needed to take action."

"What did you do?" I asked.

"Well, there was a big, burly nurse shouting questions at me," said Jeff. "She asked if I was allergic to anything. 'Yes,' I replied. The doctors and nurses stopped working as they waited for my reply. I took a deep breath and yelled, 'Bullets!' Over their laughter, I told them, 'I am choosing to live. Operate on me as if I am alive, not dead.'"

Jeff lived, thanks to the skill of his doctors but also because of his amazing attitude. I learned from him that every day we have the choice to live fully. Attitude, after all, is everything.

Application: Consider asking the following questions before continuing your sermon:

- **Do you agree with Jeff's perspective on life?**
- **When have you chosen to have a good attitude in the face of bad circumstances?**
- **How did that choice impact your life?**

....

TITLE: Under His Wings
THEME: God's protection
SCRIPTURE: Psalm 91:4
Related Passages: Psalm 28:7 and Proverbs 18:10

Story: An article in National Geographic several years ago provided a penetrating picture of God's wings. After a forest fire in Yellowstone National Park, forest rangers began their trek up a mountain to assess the inferno's damage. One ranger found a bird literally petrified in ashes, perched statuesquely on the ground at the base of a tree. Somewhat sickened by the eerie sight, he knocked over the bird with a stick. When he struck it, three tiny chicks scurried from under their dead mother's wings. The loving mother, keenly aware of impending disaster, had carried her offspring to the base of the tree and had gathered them under her wings, knowing instinctively that the toxic smoke would rise. She could have flown to safety but had refused to abandon her babies. When the blaze had arrived and the heat had singed her small body, the mother had remained steadfast. Because she had been willing to die, those under the cover of her wings would live.

Application: Consider asking the following questions before continuing your sermon:

- **Do you believe God values you in the same way the bird valued her chicks? Why or why not?**
- **What keeps you from trusting fully in God's protection in your life?**

TITLE: Big Rocks Matter Most
THEME: Priorities
SCRIPTURE: Matthew 6:33
Related Passages: Colossians 3:1-3 and Galatians 2:20

Story: One day an expert in time management was speaking to a group of business students and, to drive home a point, used an illustration those students will never forget. As he stood in front of the group of high-powered overachievers, he said, "OK, time for a quiz." Then he pulled out a one-gallon wide-mouth jar and set it on the table in front of him.

He produced about a dozen fist-sized rocks and carefully placed them, one at a time, into the jar. When the jar was filled to the top and no more rocks would fit inside, he asked, "Is this jar full?"

Everyone in the class replied, "Yes." Then he said, "Really?" He reached under the table and pulled out a bucket of gravel. Then he dumped some gravel in and shook the jar causing pieces of gravel to work themselves down into the space between the big rocks. Then he asked the group once more, "Is the jar full?"

By this time the class was on to him. "Probably not," one of them answered.

"Good!" he replied. He reached under the table and brought out a bucket of sand. He started dumping the sand in the jar, and it went into all of the spaces left between the rocks and the gravel. Once more he asked the question, "Is this jar full?"

"No!" the class shouted.

Once again he said, "Good."

Then he grabbed a pitcher of water and began to pour it in until the jar was filled to the brim. Then he looked at the class and asked, "What is the point of this illustration?" One eager beaver raised his hand and said, "The point is, no matter how full your schedule is, if you try really hard you can always fit some more things in it!"

"No," the speaker replied, "that's not the point.

Application: Consider sharing these comments before continuing your sermon:

The truth this illustration teaches us is, "If you don't put the big rocks in first, you'll never get them in at all."

What are the "big rocks" in your life? your relationship with God? time with your loved ones? your education? your dreams? a worthy cause? teaching or mentoring others? Remember to put these big rocks in first, or you'll never get them in at all.

TITLE: Modern Samaritans
THEME: Serving others
SCRIPTURE: Luke 10:30-37
Related Passages: Matthew 20:26 and Luke 22:26-27

Story: At 11:30 p.m., an older African-American woman was standing on the side of an Alabama highway trying to endure a lashing rainstorm. Her car had broken down and she desperately needed a ride. Soaking wet, she decided to flag down the next car. A young white man stopped to help her—generally unheard of in those conflict-filled 1960s. The man took her to safety, helped her get assistance, and put her into a taxi cab. She seemed to be in a big hurry! She wrote down his address, thanked him, and drove away. Seven days later, someone knocked on the man's door. To his surprise, a giant console color television was delivered to his home. A special note was attached. It read:"Thank you so much for assisting me on the highway the other night. The rain drenched not only my clothes but also my spirits. Then you came along. Because of you, I was able to make it to my dying husband's bedside just before he passed away. God bless you for helping me and unselfishly serving others."

Sincerely,

Mrs. Nat King Cole

Application: Consider asking the following questions before continuing your sermon:

- **Think of a time when you had an opportunity to serve a stranger or a friend, but you decided not to, for whatever reason. Based on this story, how might your life be different if you had decided to serve?**
- **How would your life be different if you served others as a lifestyle?**

TITLE: Remembering the Tip

THEME: Gratitude

SCRIPTURE: Luke 17:11-19

Related Passage: Colossians 2:7

Story: In the days when an ice-cream sundae cost much less, a ten-year-old boy entered a hotel coffee shop and sat at a table. A waitress put a glass of water in front of him. "How much is an ice cream sundae?" he asked.

"Fifty cents," replied the waitress. The little boy pulled his hand out of his pocket and studied a number of coins in it.

"How much is a dish of plain ice cream?" he inquired. Some other people were now waiting for a table, and the waitress was a bit impatient. "Thirty-five cents," she said brusquely. The little boy again counted the coins. "I'll have the plain ice cream," he said. The waitress brought the ice cream, put the bill on the table, and walked away. The boy finished the ice cream, paid the cashier, and departed.

When the waitress came back, she began wiping down the table and then swallowed hard at what she saw. There, placed neatly beside the empty dish, were two nickels and five pennies—her tip.

Application: Consider asking the following questions before continuing your sermon:

- **When have you been impacted by another person's unexpected gratitude toward you for something you did?**
- **How can you show more gratitude to others in everyday life?**

TITLE: Blood Sacrifice

THEME: Sacrificial love

SCRIPTURE: Luke 23:26-49

Related Passages: Ephesians 1:7 and Colossians 1:20

Story: Many years ago, a young woman was working as a volunteer at Stanford Hospital. While she was there, she got to know a little girl named Liz who was suffering from a rare and serious disease. Her only chance of recovery appeared to be a blood transfusion from her five-year-old brother, who had miraculously survived the same disease and had developed the antibodies needed to combat the illness.

The doctor explained the situation to her little brother and asked the boy if he would be willing to give his blood to his sister. He hesitated for only a moment before taking a deep breath and saying, "Yes, I'll do it if it will save Liz." As the transfusion progressed, he lay in bed next to his sister and smiled, seeing the color returning to her cheeks. Then his face grew pale and his smile faded. He looked up at the doctor and asked with a trembling voice, "Will I start to die right away?"

Being young, the boy had misunderstood the doctor; he thought he was going to have to give his sister all of his blood.

Application: Consider asking the following questions before continuing your sermon:

- **Do you know anyone who is willing to die for you? How does that make you feel?**
- **How is the little boy's sacrifice for his sister like Jesus' sacrifice for us?**
- **Why is it so important that love be expressed in sacrificial ways?**

TITLE: The King Is Watching
THEME: Life's struggles
SCRIPTURE: Matthew 6:1
Related Passages: Matthew 6:19 and Colossians 3:23

Story: In ancient times, a king had a boulder placed on a roadway. Then he hid and watched to see if anyone would remove the huge rock. Some of the king's wealthiest merchants and courtiers came by and simply walked around it. Many loudly blamed the king for not keeping the roads clear, but none did anything about getting the stone out of the way.

Then a peasant came along, carrying a load of vegetables. Approaching the boulder, the peasant laid down his burden and tried to move the stone to the side of the road. After much pushing and straining, he finally succeeded. As the peasant picked up his load of vegetables, he noticed a purse lying in the road where the boulder had been. The purse contained many gold coins and a note from the king indicating that the gold was for the person who removed the boulder from the roadway. The peasant learned what many others never understand. Every obstacle presents an opportunity to improve one's condition.

Application: Consider asking the following questions before continuing your sermon:

- **What's one "boulder" in the road of your life right now?**
- **Do you see that boulder as an opportunity to grow? Why or why not?**

....

TITLE: On the Brink of Life and Death
THEME: Salvation
SCRIPTURE: Matthew 4:17
Related Passages: Acts 2:38-39; Romans 1:16-17; and 1 Corinthians 1:18

Story: This story is told by a Christian who was a student at the University of Cincinnati in 1967.

While taking a class in photography at the University of Cincinnati, I became acquainted with a young man named Charles Murray, who was a fellow student at the university and was also training as a high diver for the summer Olympics of 1968. Charles was very patient with me as I spoke to him for hours about Jesus Christ and how he had saved me. Charles was not raised in a family that attended any kind of church, so all that I had to tell him was fascinating to him. He even began to ask questions about forgiveness of sin.

Finally, the day came that I put a question to him. I asked if he realized his own need of a Redeemer and if he was ready to trust Christ as his own Savior. I saw his countenance fall and the guilt in his face. But his reply was a strong "No."

In the days that followed, he was quiet, and often I felt that he was avoiding me until I got a phone call and it was Charles. He wanted to know where to look in the New Testament for some verses that I had given him about salvation. I gave him the reference to several passages and asked if I could meet with him. He declined my offer and thanked me for the Scripture. I could tell that he was greatly troubled, but I didn't know where he was or how to help him.

Because he was training for the Olympic games, Charles had special privileges at the university pool facilities. Some time between 10:30 and 11:00 that evening he decided to swim and practice a few dives. It was a clear night in October and the moon was big and bright. The university pool was housed under a ceiling of glass panes so the moon shone brightly across the top of the wall in the pool area.

Charles climbed to the highest platform to take his first dive. At that moment the Spirit of God began to convict him of his sins. All the Scripture he had read, all the occasions of my witnessing to him about Christ flooded his mind.

He stood on the platform backwards to make his dive, spread his arms to gather his balance, looked up to the wall, and saw his own shadow caused by the light of the moon. It was the shape of a cross. He could bear the burden of his sin no longer. His heart broke, and he sat down on the platform and asked God to forgive him and save him. He trusted Jesus Christ twenty-some feet in the air.

Suddenly the lights in the pool area came on. The attendant had come in to check the pool. As Charles looked down from his platform, he saw an empty pool that had been drained for repairs. He had almost plummeted to his death, but the cross had saved him from disaster.

Application: Consider asking the following questions before continuing your sermon:

- **Why do you think people resist the good news of Christ's salvation?**
- **Who do you know that needs to hear this message?**
- **Have you told them? Why or why not?**

TITLE: Jesus 1.0
THEME: Christian growth
SCRIPTURE: Romans 12:1-2
Related Passages: 2 Corinthians 5:17 and Galatians 2:20

Story: I am writing because of questions from people regarding installation of the latest version of the popular program Jesus 1.0 (also available as Yeshua 1.0). It seems that installation of Jesus 1.0 eventually leads to several conflicts with other programs you may be running and may even require certain upgrades and utility programs.

Jesus 1.0 usually installs easily enough. The program has been around for years and was written so well that it has never needed to be upgraded. It runs on the oldest of machines as well as on the fanciest of operating systems running at blazing speed. System requirements are minimal. Jesus 1.0 requires virtually no RAM initially and is self-installing. The evaluation copy and full version are available free of charge, despite reportedly enormous development costs.

Problems arise, however, as you use the program. Jesus 1.0 runs in the background and does a systematic evaluation of all programs, utilities, and games on your system. For example, Jesus 1.0 does not run well at all with Religion 1.0 and higher or Hate 1.0. There are extreme conflicts with these and other programs that are unresolvable. Jesus 1.0 also evaluates network connections that may be dangerous. Jesus 1.0 uses pop-up windows to suggest better utilization of disk space by deleting old programs and routines as well as severing dangerous network connections. This is actually very helpful, and responding will result in extremely efficient and productive use of your system.

When installing Jesus 1.0, you should be aware that when a pop-up window makes a suggestion to remove a program or routine, there is no choice on the pop-up that says, "Do not show this warning again." Some feel this is a flaw in the system because they cannot remove these persistent warnings. The warnings actually become more urgent, such as, "Continued use of Program XYZ or Game ABC may result in a fatal error or permanent damage to your system." (Note: Jesus 1.0 does not uninstall easily, if at all. Software engineers debate whether this is even possible.)

Removing old programs at the suggestion of Jesus 1.0 can be difficult, so we recommend a powerful utility program called HolySpirit 1.0. HolySpirit 1.0 is capable of removing any program that is in conflict with the smooth operation of Jesus 1.0 while also sweeping for viruses. HolySpirit 1.0 is actually a utility that comes with Jesus 1.0 but often needs to be installed or unzipped (though some report that it self-installs automatically).

HolySpirit 1.0 can be a bit of a memory hog and is a little unpredictable. It can even make the system appear unstable for brief periods of time. HolySpirit 1.0 makes Jesus 1.0 run at lightning speed on any operating system and debugs your communications software. It is really quite marvelous and runs as a memory-resident program.

We have found that HolySpirit 1.0 runs best in conjunction with any of the popular HisWord software programs available from Yahweh. HisWord is an extensive online manual that also automatically repairs broken files, clusters, and strings of data. HisWord is available in various versions, such as KJV, NAS, NIV, and so on. The program is in the public domain and is available at modest cost.

You also may have heard that there is a powerful utility command available in Jesus 1.0 called Repent.exe. Repent.exe does not install as a shortcut. The command causes an intensive reworking of your entire system, somewhat like a soft reformat. All illegal and pirated programs are deleted, sleeping viruses are purged, and all software is updated. Repent.exe is an extreme command that causes an evaluation and virtual rewrite of your system item by item, but the results are terrific.

Bottom line, we view Jesus 1.0 as an essential program that we highly recommend, especially with use of HolySpirit 1.0 and HisWord 1.0.

Application: Consider asking the following questions before continuing your sermon:

- **What has surprised you most about the changes God has accomplished in your heart?**
- **In what areas of your life are you still resisting God's efforts to change you?**
- **How would your life be different if you "erased" your own program and allowed God to take over your life completely?**

SCRIPTURE INDEX

THEME INDEX